The Enneagram Code

Understanding Personality Types for Better Relationships

Eden Storm

© **Copyright 2023 - All rights reserved.**

The content contained within this book may not be reproduced, duplicated, or transmitted without direct written permission from the author or the publisher.

Under no circumstances will any blame or legal responsibility be held against the publisher, or author, for any damages, reparation, or monetary loss due to the information contained within this book, either directly or indirectly.

Legal Notice:

This book is copyright protected. It is only for personal use. You cannot amend, distribute, sell, use, quote or paraphrase any part, or the content within this book, without the consent of the author or publisher.

Disclaimer Notice:

Please note the information contained within this document is for educational and entertainment purposes only. All effort has been executed to present accurate, up to date, reliable, complete information. No warranties of any kind are declared or implied. Readers acknowledge that the author is not engaged in the rendering of legal, financial, medical, or professional advice. The content within this book has been derived from various sources. Please consult a licensed professional before attempting any techniques outlined in this book.

By reading this document, the reader agrees that under no circumstances is the author responsible for any losses, direct or indirect, that are incurred as a result of the use of the information contained within this document, including, but not limited to, errors, omissions, or inaccuracies.

Enhance Your Enneagram Experience!

Unlock the secrets of 'The Enneagram Code' with your complimentary easy-reference guide to the nine Enneagram personality types.

Simply scan the QR code, follow the instructions, and print off your personal guide to carry with you through your enlightening journey.

Understand yourself and others like never before, making every page of the book an even more insightful experience. Get ready to embrace a new level of self-awareness and stronger, more empathetic relationships – claim your free guide now!

Table of Contents

Introduction 1

Chapter 1: Understanding the Enneagram 5

   The Modern History of the Enneagram 7
      The Enneagram Symbol 9

   The Nine Enneagram Personality Types 10
      1. The Perfectionist/Reformer 10
      2. The Helper/Giver 12
      3. The Achiever/Performer 14
      4. The Individualist/Romantic 17
      5. The Investigator/Observer 19
      6. The Loyalist/Skeptic 21
      7. The Enthusiast/Epicure 23
      8. The Challenger/Protector 25
      9. The Peacemaker/Mediator 27

   Wings, Subtypes, and Levels of Health 29
      Enneagram Wings 30
      Subtypes 30
      Levels of Development, or Health Within the Enneagram Type 34

   How to Gain Self-Awareness by Using the Enneagram 35
      Using the Enneagram to Gain Self-Awareness—Jean's Story 36

   Practical Journal Activity: Determine Your Enneagram Type 38
      Reflection 39
      Activities 39

   Key Takeaways 40

Chapter 2: The System for Understanding Personality Types for Better Relationships **45**

Overview of the Psychological Theory of the Enneagram 46
How the Enneagram Helped Me Develop More Compassion with Others 48

How the Enneagram Can Help People Recognize and Overcome Their Obstacles 49

Growth Paths for the Different Enneagram Types ..51
Type 1—The Perfectionist/Reformer 51
Type 2—The Helper/Giver 52
Type 3—The Achiever/Performer 53
Type 4—The Individualist/Romantic 54
Type 5—The Investigator/Observer 55
Type 6—The Loyalist/Skeptic 57
Type 7—The Enthusiast/Epicure 59
Type 8—The Challenger/Protector 61
Type 9—The Peacemaker/Mediator 63
The Enneagram Encourages Personal Challenges—Mia's Story 65

Practical Exercise—Explore Your Enneagram Type 68

Key Takeaways 70

Chapter 3: Identify Your Personality Type **73**

Using the Enneagram to Determine Your Personality Type 74
How Childhood Memories and Experiences Can Affect Your Enneagram Type 75
How Childhood Trauma Could Have Affected Your Personality Type 77

Self-Evaluation Techniques That Can Help You Determine Your Enneagram Type 80
Examples of How the Enneagram Has Helped People Improve Their Relationships 82

Compatible Enneagram Types 84
    Which Enneagram Types Are More Compatible? 85
    Which Are the Least Compatible Types? 86
    Strategies to Overcome Compatibility Challenges 88
    How People from Different Enneagram Types Overcame Their Challenges 90

Detailed Description of the Different Enneagram Types 92
    1. The Perfectionist/Reformer 92
    2. The Helper/Giver 94
    3. Achiever/Performer 97
    4. Individualist/Romantic 99
    5. Investigator/Observer 101
    6. The Loyalist/Skeptic 103
    7. The Enthusiast/Epicure 106
    8. The Challenger/Protector 110
    9. The Peacemaker/Mediator 113

Practical Exercise: Improve Communication with the Different Enneagram Types 116
    Instructions 116

Key Takeaways 118

Chapter 4: Improving Personal and Professional Relationships 121

The Benefit of the Enneagram for Professional Teams 122

How the Different Enneagram Types Approach Their Work and Relationships 124
    Type 1—The Perfectionist/Reformer 124
    Type 2—The Helper/Giver 126
    Type 3—The Achiever/Performer 127
    Type 4—The Individualist/Romantic 128
    Type 5—The Investigator/Observer 129
    Type 6—The Loyalist/Skeptic 131
    Type 7—The Enthusiast/Epicure 132
    Type 8—The Challenger/Protector 133
    Type 9—The Peacemaker/Mediator 134

Ideal Job Roles for the Different Enneagram Types 135
- Type 1—The Perfectionist/Reformer 135
- Type 2—The Helper/Giver 137
- Type 3—The Achiever/Performer...................................... 138
- Type 4—The Individualist/Romantic................................. 139
- Type 5—The Investigator/Observer 140
- Type 6—The Loyalist/Skeptic 141
- Type 7—The Enthusiast/Epicure 142
- Type 8—The Challenger/Protector 143
- Type 9—The Peacemaker/Mediator.................................. 144

How Using the Enneagram Can Increase Job Satisfaction 146

How the Enneagram Helped People from Different Backgrounds to Work Together 148

Personality Tests in the Workplace 150
- Activity—A Combination of Personality Tests for the Workplace 151

Practical Exercise—Enneagram Activities That Can Help You Develop Your Team 154
- Activities.. 155

Key Takeaways 156

Chapter 5: Applying the Enneagram in Your Life. 159

Reasons to Learn More About Your Enneagram Type 161
- Mindfulness and the Enneagram 164
- How to Use the Enneagram When You Fear Personal Change.. 167
- The Enneagram Can Help You Identify and Release Patterns of Self-Judgment and Negative Self-Talk 169

Developing a Personalized Enneagram-Based Personal Growth Plan: Tools and Resources 170

Using the Enneagram in Conjunction with Other Tests 172
- Myers-Briggs Type Indicator 172

Big Five Personality Traits 173
Activity—Building Your Own Enneagram Growth Plan 176
    Reflection 177
    Growth Areas 177
    Growth Goals 177
    Planning 178
    Self-Accountability 178
    Reflection and Commitment 178

Key Takeaways 179

Conclusion 181

About the Author 185

References 189

Introduction

Have you always thought of yourself as being open-minded, and you always got along with most people in your life? Then, all of a sudden, someone comes into your life who you can't stand, and you're not really sure why?

Maybe there's something about this person that you just can't seem to grasp. They're different from you in every possible way, and the more you try to understand them, the more frustrated you become. Yet, there is something about them that leaves you wanting to know more about them.

Their mannerisms, their beliefs, their way of life—all very different from your own. It's as if they come from an entirely different world.

You get involved in a heated argument with them where you try to make them see your point of view, using rational arguments and facts. But their response is laced with emotion and personal experiences. It feels like you're speaking two different languages, and you start to feel like the gap between you can't be bridged.

You lose your patience and end up having a full-blown fight with this person, where you hurl serious insults at one another. As the dust settles, you start to regret your actions and words. You're still curious about this person, but now you feel that a bridge has been created between you that can't be crossed.

You realize that while you've always prided yourself in embracing diversity and appreciating different perspectives, you're going to need something more to help you understand others. You're going to have to find the patience and compassion to connect to others on a deeper level.

That's where the Enneagram can come in handy: to give you a more in-depth understanding of all the people in your life.

The aim of this book is to give you a better understanding of the Enneagram system and how it can be used to understand human personalities. The Enneagram is a powerful tool that can help you with personal growth. It can help you understand the people in your life better and improve your communication and relationships with them.

The book also introduces you to the Enneagram's nine different personality types, which each have their own ways of thinking, feeling, and behaving. The motivations, fears, desires, and core beliefs of each type will be considered, shedding light on the dynamics that shape our thoughts and behavior.

From a personal perspective, the Enneagram has helped me with self-reflection and understanding. Knowing my Enneagram type has also given me insight into the way I behave, as well as my motivation for behaving in certain ways.

Knowing and understanding my Enneagram type has also helped me determine my fears and desires. I have come to see how they influence my decision-making and self-perception, and, in turn, my relationships. It helped me understand in which areas I should focus on personal growth and how I could break free from limiting patterns.

The Enneagram has also given me more empathy for the people in my life, as well as a more profound understanding of their behavior and personalities. By understanding their perspectives according to their Enneagram types, I developed an appreciation of their challenges, as well as their strengths. I have been able to develop better communication skills, which has also allowed me to approach conflicts with more understanding.

My ongoing experience with the Enneagram continues to help me gain greater self-awareness, which has helped me a great deal when it comes to personal growth. It continues to guide me on my ongoing journey of self-discovery.

The Enneagram can ultimately contribute to your personal fulfillment. You can lead a more purposeful life by being your authentic self and acting in a way that aligns with your core values. The Enneagram will empower you to make the type of decisions and choices that will help you reach your goals and give you a greater sense of satisfaction with your life.

Although the Enneagram is a fantastic tool for self-discovery and personal growth, people's experiences may differ. It is important to remember that to get the full benefit of the Enneagram, you should be willing to be an active participant in your personal growth, partake in self-reflection, and have a lifelong learning mentality.

Chapter 1:

Understanding the Enneagram

A while back, somewhere in a bustling city in the modern world, lived an intelligent and curious woman called Rosa. She had an insatiable thirst for knowledge and loved psychology. The biggest and most exciting challenge in her life was trying to understand the intricacies of the human mind.

One day, she discovered a dusty old bookstore hidden away in a forgotten corner of the city. While looking through the dimly lit shelves, she found a worn-out book that appeared to be about the Enneagram and unlocking the secrets of your personality.

Rosa was intrigued, and she began to read the book. She was captivated by this ancient system's promise of self-discovery and personal growth. She wanted to know more and embarked on a journey to discover more about the history of the Enneagram.

She discovered that the Enneagram could trace back its history for several centuries and that it had originated from ancient wisdom and spiritual teachings.

Rosa attended workshops and seminars that were offered by experts who were dedicated to unraveling the Enneagram's mysteries.

She wanted to share the transformative power of the Enneagram that she had discovered with others. She hosted gatherings in her apartment and invited her friends and other acquaintances to explore and discover their own Enneagram types. The response was overwhelming, and her friends discovered a deep sense of connection with one another, as well as a newfound sense of self-awareness.

Rosa's informal gatherings eventually blossomed into an official group, with more and more people joining her meetings. The group moved to a coffee shop and eventually to a community center. Rosa's group spread the word, and they eventually became a beacon of hope for people who wanted to achieve self-understanding and connection.

As time passes, even in the modern world, more people are becoming interested in increasing their self-awareness by using the Enneagram, an ancient tool of enlightenment.

The Enneagram has a long and complex history over different spiritual, psychological, and philosophical traditions.

Its roots can be traced back to the ancient civilizations of the Babylonians, Egyptians, and Greeks. Symbolic diagrams that resemble the Enneagram figure are found in various spiritual and mystical traditions, representing universal patterns of creation and interconnectedness.

The Modern History of the Enneagram

The modern Enneagram is largely the result of the work of certain key figures:

- George Ivanovich Gurdjieff (1866–1949), a philosopher and spiritual teacher, introduced the Enneagram symbol to the western world in the early 20th century. He used it to teach psychological and spiritual insights, emphasizing the need for self-awareness and personal transformation.

- Oscar Ichazo (1931–2020) built on Gurdjieff's teachings and developed a system of nine personality types connected to the Enneagram symbol. He focused on the psychological aspects of the Enneagram and linked each type to distinct motivations, fixations, and behavioral patterns.

- Claudio Naranjo (1932–2019), a psychiatrist and student of Ichazo, further developed the Enneagram system. He integrated psychological and therapeutic insights and expanded the understanding of the Enneagram types and their relationship to personal growth and self awareness.

The nine Enneagram personality types play a crucial role in the modern history of the Enneagram. It has shaped how people apply and understand this tool. As the Enneagram gained popularity and expanded into the modern world, these nine distinct types became a fundamental framework for self-discovery, personal growth, and enhancing relationships.

Each Enneagram type represents a unique set of patterns, motivations, and fears, offering a deep dive into the complexities of human personality. They provide a road map for individuals to explore their core motivations, defense mechanisms, and growth opportunities.

In the context of modern history, the nine Enneagram types have become a language for understanding ourselves and others. They offer a lens through which we can view others, and which allows us to empathize with different perspectives and appreciate the diverse ways people find their way through the world.

As the Enneagram gained increasing popularity, researchers, psychologists, and enthusiasts delved deeper into each type, shedding light on their distinct characteristics, strengths, and challenges. This knowledge has contributed to the development of comprehensive descriptions, which allowed people to identify their own Enneagram types and embark on a journey of self-awareness.

In the digital age, the nine Enneagram types have also become a central theme in online communities, social media platforms, and Enneagram-focused websites. People share experiences and seek guidance from others who share their Enneagram type, creating a sense of community and support.

The Enneagram's modern history is intertwined with the understanding and exploration of the nine personality types. They serve as the foundation for personal growth, self-reflection, and building bridges between individuals in an increasingly interconnected world. By embracing the power of the nine types, we can deepen our understanding of ourselves and cultivate meaningful relationships.

The Enneagram Symbol

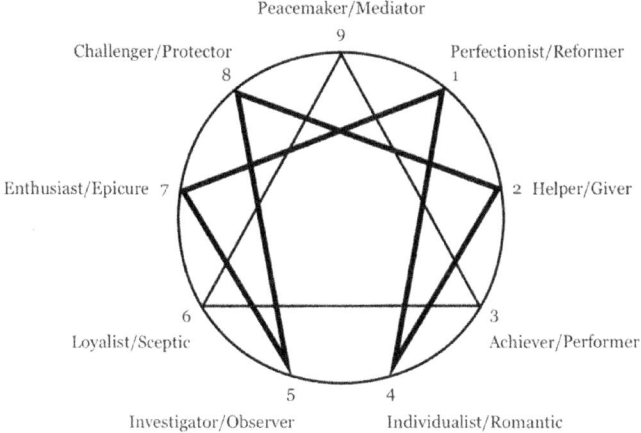

The Nine Enneagram Personality Types

Each of the nine Enneagram types represents a different way of feeling, thinking, and behaving.

1. The Perfectionist/Reformer

The first Enneagram type is rational, idealistic, and strives for perfection. Their aim is to improve themselves and those around them.

They can have the following personality characteristics:

- This personality type has a desire to create order and structure. They also have high standards for themselves and others.

- The Reformer also has a strong sense of integrity and a firm moral compass. They value honesty, ethics, and strive to live according to their principles.

- Reformers tend to be very critical of themselves. They have an inner critic that constantly pushes them to improve themselves, and their judgment of themselves can be harsh when they don't achieve something.

- The Reformer is also detail-oriented, and they're excellent at spotting inconsistencies and mistakes. They value things being done correctly. These are the types of people that are excellent editors or proofreaders.

- As a result of their inner drive for improvement, Type 1s can be super-focused on improving themselves and the world at large. They can see areas for correction, and they may feel that it's part of their responsibility to make things better.

- Type 1s could also struggle with perfectionism, which could be frustrating for them. They could end up feeling nothing they do is good enough.

- They could find it difficult to delegate tasks to others or let go since they have a strong need to control their environment.

- Reformers have a strong sense of justice and fairness. They could work in areas they feel passionate about in roles as advocates, reformers, or activists.

- They could also feel as if they need to work on improving their relationships. They have high expectations of themselves and their partners in relationships.

Growth Recommendations

The Reformer can do the following to improve their lives:

- They have to realize that they can't save the whole world and that they need to make time for themselves and to relax.

- Reformers need to get in touch with their emotions and become more comfortable with them. It could benefit them to keep a journal to work through their emotions.

- Reformers enjoy teaching and helping others, but they shouldn't expect things to be as obvious to others as they are to them, or that other people should be able to change immediately.

- They could get upset and angry easily when others refuse to do what they see as the right thing. They need to realize that their anger could alienate others and that it would put others off from the good things that they're trying to say. Repressed anger is also bad for their own health.

2. *The Helper/Giver*

The Helper, or the Giver, is the second type on the Enneagram. The core desire of this type is to be loved and appreciated. They love meeting new people and making a positive impact on them. The Helper wants to be of service to others, often at the expense of their own well-being.

Their personality characteristics are as follows:

- Helpers are caring and empathetic. They want to alleviate the suffering of others and make them feel loved. They're great at providing emotional support to everyone around them.

- Helpers tend to be selfless and put the needs of others above their own. They overextend themselves, as they often ignore their own needs and feelings.

- They are generous and feel joy in meeting the needs of those they care about.

- Helpers can sense the needs and emotions of those around them. They can pick up on subtle cues and can offer the right support and guidance.

- Givers, or Helpers, may also have a need for appreciation and for acknowledgment of their efforts. They might ignore their own self-worth as they seek external validation.

- Helpers could fear being rejected or unloved and try to avoid conflicts at all costs.

- Helpers/Givers do well in close relationships, as they put a lot of energy into them. They work hard at creating harmonious interactions with others.

Growth Recommendations

Helpers can do the following to improve their lives:

- Helpers need to learn to address their own needs, otherwise they will become frustrated and start to feel resentful. They need to take care of themselves properly, for example, by eating well and sleeping enough, to make sure they don't get overwhelmed by the needs of others.

- Helpers should also ask people if they really need the help they want to give them. A Helper can see where help is needed, but that doesn't necessarily mean someone wants their help.

- When deciding to help someone, the Helper also needs to be aware of their motives. They should keep in mind that they could be disappointed if they're expecting others to do good things for them in return.

3. *The Achiever/Performer*

The Achiever, also known as the Performer, is typically associated with Enneagram Type 3. Individuals of this type have a core desire to be successful, valued, and admired. They have a strong motivation to achieve their goals and to stand out in their chosen field. The Achiever's primary focus is to accomplish tasks and get recognition for them.

The Achiever's personality characteristics are as follows:

- Achievers are driven individuals who set ambitious goals for themselves. They have a strong desire to succeed, and they usually have a clear vision of what they want to achieve. They work hard to make sure their goals become a reality.

- Achievers, or Performers, are conscious of their public image and always try to present themselves in a positive light. They pay attention to how others perceive them and work hard to maintain a successful and polished appearance.

- Achievers are energetic and enthusiastic individuals. They bring a sense of vitality and passion to their pursuits, which can inspire those around them. They excel in dynamic and fast-paced environments.

- The Achiever/Performer is a flexible personality type that can adapt to different situations. They have a natural ability to assess what is required and they can change their approaches accordingly. This versatility allows them to excel in various roles and environments.

- Achievers are focused on tangible outcomes and measurable achievements. They set high standards for themselves and constantly seek validation through their accomplishments. They thrive on recognition and praise for their efforts.

- They always try to protect their image and reputation. They are often mindful of the opinions and judgments of others and may at times feel pressure to maintain a flawless image.

- The Achiever strives for excellence in all that they do. They have a natural inclination to improve their skills, expand their knowledge, and outperform their peers. They enjoy being in competitive environments.

- Achievers/Performers can become workaholics, constantly pushing themselves to accomplish more and take on additional responsibilities. They may struggle with maintaining a work-life balance, and it's difficult for them to slow down and relax.

- Achievers/Performers derive a sense of worth and identity from being acknowledged and admired by others. However, they may sometimes struggle with a fear of failure.

Growth Recommendations

Achievers can try the following to improve their lives:

- Achievers should try to be more authentic and not try to impress others by inflating their own importance.

- Achievers should also take breaks to reconnect with themselves.

4. *The Individualist/Romantic*

The Individualist, also called the Romantic or Enneagram Type 4, is associated with introspective and creative people who want to live authentic, meaningful lives. They also want to experience profound emotional depth and establish their own unique identities.

The personality characteristics of this type are as follows:

- This type is attuned to their emotions and has a rich inner world. They can experience their emotions more intensely than others, which also fuels their creativity and gives them a unique perspective on life.

- They want to be genuine and authentic and may struggle to conform to societal expectations. They want to find and express their own unique identity.

- The idealism of the Individualist also draws them to artistic and creative activities. They look for beauty and meaning in everything in their lives.

- As Individualists, they want to stand out in the crowd. They can have a talent or a distinct personal style that sets them apart from others. As self-aware individuals, they enjoy exploring their own thoughts and feelings.

- When it comes to emotions, they can experience intense highs and lows. They are emotionally sensitive and can empathize with others.

- The Individualist fears being ordinary, and that people won't understand who they are. They can look for recognition or validation from others.

- Individualists want to make meaningful connections with others. They enjoy emotional intimacy and prefer being with people who can appreciate their individuality and who want to engage in heartfelt conversations.

Growth Recommendations

- Individualists should pay less attention to their feelings. They should accept that they are not their feelings and that their feelings are only telling them something about themselves in the present moment.

- They should commit themselves to doing productive work and avoid putting important projects off until they are in the right mood.

- Individualists need to put themselves out there and take on challenges, even if they feel they're not ready to do so. Positive experiences will help them develop their self-esteem.

- Individualists should try to maintain routines and self-discipline.

5. The Investigator/Observer

Type 5 on the Enneagram, namely the Investigator or Observer, is an analytical person who wants to understand the world and gain more knowledge about it.

Their personal characteristics are as follows:

- Investigators want to observe and analyze their surroundings. Their analytical mindset helps them understand and interpret information.

- They are eager learners who always want to learn more, explore different ideas, and increase their understanding of different subjects.

- They usually remain objective and detached when they interact with people. They are reserved when expressing emotion and don't always want to share their emotional experiences with others. They approach situations with logical reasoning and intellectual curiosity.

- They are private people who value their personal space. They are also introspective and need time alone to recharge.

- Investigators will prioritize knowledge and intellectual pursuits above wealth. Gathering new ideas is more important to them than getting rich.

- Investigators aim to become experts in the areas that interest them. They want to become authorities in their fields.

Growth Recommendations

The Investigator/Observer can grow in the following areas:

- Investigators should try not to live too much in their minds and rather stay more connected with the physical aspects of their existence.

- Investigators should try to relax and live in a calmer, healthier way, without turning to unhealthy mechanisms such as drugs or alcohol. Exercises such as meditation, yoga, dancing, and jogging can be useful ways of unwinding for this type.

- Investigators shouldn't allow themselves to be distracted from what they are really meant to do. They have a tendency to get involved in projects that don't necessarily support their goals and self-esteem.

6. The Loyalist/Skeptic

Loyalists are committed and responsible individuals who seek security and support. They can be cautious and anxious. They also have a tendency to anticipate potential problems.

Their personal characteristics are as follows:

- Loyalists are loyal and committed to their relationships and beliefs. They value trust and reliability, and they are supportive of those they care about.

- The primary motivation of Loyalists is to feel secure and protected. They seek stability and predictability in their lives and are often cautious and risk-averse in their decision-making.

- Loyalists can anticipate potential problems and risks. They are vigilant and alert, and they constantly scan their environment for threats or challenges.

- They may have a constant need for reassurance and validation from others. Loyalists will seek guidance and support to alleviate their anxieties and gain a sense of security.

- They are also skeptical and questioning. They tend to challenge information and authority and usually consider multiple perspectives and gather evidence before they make decisions or form beliefs.

- Loyalists could also have higher levels of anxiety compared to other personality types. They can be worriers and anticipate future difficulties.

- Loyalists want the safety and support of belonging to a group. They find comfort in being part of a community or in having a strong support system.

- Loyalists are protective of their loved ones and the causes they believe in. They could become vocal advocates for justice and fairness, and they fight against perceived threats or injustices.

- They could also struggle with trusting others easily. They may have a cautious approach to forming new relationships and may take time to establish trust due to their fear of betrayal or disappointment.

- Loyalists are often prepared and diligent planners. They anticipate potential challenges and make contingency plans to ensure their safety and security.

Growth Recommendations

Loyalists can grow in the following areas:

- Loyalists should focus on becoming aware of when they become stressed and anxious. They should deal with their stress via healthy coping mechanisms, such as by doing enough exercise.
- They should work at not blaming themselves or others when they become upset and angry.
- They should work harder at trusting others.

7. The Enthusiast/Epicure

The Enthusiast, also called the Epicure, is adventurous and spontaneous and is usually looking for stimulation and new experiences.

Their personal characteristics are as follows:

- Enthusiasts have a zest for life and are always looking for new adventures. They tend to look for excitement and novelty. They enjoy environments that offer variety and new possibilities.

- This Enthusiast is optimistic and has a positive outlook on life. They're capable of inspiring those around them with their enthusiasm and infectious energy.

- They are usually interested in many different activities. Enthusiasts enjoy exploring different hobbies, ideas, and perspectives, embracing the diversity of life.

- Enthusiasts can have a fear of missing out on exciting experiences or opportunities. This fear drives them to constantly seek stimulation and keep themselves engaged in various activities.

- This type actively seeks pleasure and enjoyment in life. They are often drawn to pleasurable experiences, such as good food, travel, entertainment, and social events.

- The Enthusiast has a quick and agile mind that generates ideas and possibilities effortlessly. They are often good at brainstorming and coming up with creative ideas spontaneously.

- They tend to distract themselves from negative emotions or challenging situations. The Enthusiast prefers to focus on positive experiences and may either avoid or minimize dealing with discomfort or pain.

- This type has a fear of being trapped or restricted. They resist anything that may limit their freedom or stop them from enjoying life to the fullest.

- Enthusiasts can struggle with commitment and may be prone to restlessness. They may have a fear of being tied down or missing out on other opportunities, leading to a constant search for new experiences.

Growth Recommendations

Enthusiasts can grow in the following areas:

- Enthusiasts need to learn to recognize and question their impulses without just giving in and acting on them.

- This type needs to learn to listen to other people and learn from them. Their growth area is to learn to live with less external stimulation.

- They also need to think about the long-term consequences of what they want to do.

8. *The Challenger/Protector*

Type 8, the Challenger, is an assertive, confident, and strong-willed individual who values control and independence. They have a desire to protect the vulnerable and fight against injustice.

The personal characteristics of the Challenger are as follows:

- They are assertive and strong-willed. They will voice their opinions and stand up for what they believe in. They will strive to maintain their autonomy.

- They are loyal and want to protect those they care about. They want to defend and protect the rights of others.

- They are passionate and courageous and will confront challenges head-on. They inspire others with their fearlessness.

- The Challenger communicates directly and assertively. They appreciate honesty and direct communication.

- The Challenger can be intense and prone to anger. They can react strongly to situations they see as unfair.

- They aren't afraid to confront difficult situations or people when necessary. They are direct in addressing conflicts or issues that arise and may be confrontational when they feel their values are being compromised.

- Challengers fear appearing weak or vulnerable. They strive to maintain a strong and confident exterior and may find it difficult to show vulnerability or ask for support.

Growth Areas

The Challenger can grow in the following areas:

- The self-confident and willful Challenger needs to learn to react with self-restraint. They are at their best when it comes to inspiring others and helping them through a crisis.

- The Challenger also needs to learn that they occasionally need to yield to others and that they don't have to dominate all the time.

- Challengers need to accept that others aren't against them and that they should show appreciation for the people they have in their lives.

- They should also learn to understand that people who value them for their power don't always love them for who they really are.

9. The Peacemaker/Mediator

The Peacemaker is easygoing and tends to avoid conflict. They are driven by a desire for inner and outer harmony.

Their personal characteristics are as follows:

- Peacemakers tend to have a calm and easygoing demeanor. They prefer to go with the flow and avoid conflicts or disruptions. They strive to keep their relationships peaceful and harmonious.

- The primary motivation of Peacemakers is to avoid conflict and cultivate a sense of inner and outer peace. They value tranquility, balance, and a sense of serenity in their lives and interactions.

- They may find it challenging to confront others or express their own needs and desires, choosing instead to keep the peace and maintain a sense of harmony. They usually prioritize the needs of others above their own.

- They make great mediators or peacekeepers in conflicts, striving to find common ground and facilitate understanding between others.

- They are often adaptable and flexible and can adjust their preferences and accommodate the needs of others.

- Peacemakers may struggle with making decisions, as they often consider multiple perspectives and strive to find the option that will lead to the least amount of conflict or disruption.

- They can find it difficult to express anger. They may suppress or internalize their frustrations to prevent conflict, but this can lead to a buildup of resentment over time.

- Peacemakers value connection and acceptance from others. They seek to create a sense of belonging and harmony in their relationships and are often skilled at creating a peaceful and inclusive atmosphere.

Growth Areas

Peacemakers can grow in the following areas:

- Peacemakers need to re-examine their tendency to go along with the wishes of others. They need to become more emotionally engaged, exert themselves, and take part in life.

- They need to work at expressing their own needs and desires and realize that they are also important.

- Peacemakers need to learn to express their negative emotions, such as anxiety and anger, and deal with them. They need to get more in touch with these feelings.

- They need to recognize how regular exercise can help them get more in touch with their bodies and emotions.

Wings, Subtypes, and Levels of Health

You can further understand your Enneagram type by looking at its wings, subtypes, and levels of health.

Enneagram Wings

The wings are the adjacent personality types that influence and complement your core personality. The wings can enhance or diminish your personality traits.

For example, if you're a Type 4, your wings could be Type 3 or Type 5. The traits from these types can also shape your personality and behavior.

The influence will also be different from person to person. Some people might be more influenced by one wing, while others may have a more balanced influence from both wings. The wings can be seen as a continuum, with the dominant Enneagram type representing the core and the wings adding different traits.

The wing types can give you additional insight into your motivations, fears, and desires. If you explore the characteristics and tendencies of the adjacent wings, you could gain a more comprehensive understanding of your Enneagram type.

Understanding and integrating the influence of the wings can also help you gain greater self-awareness and contribute to your personal growth.

Subtypes

The Enneagram subtypes are also known as "instinctual variants" and refer to three different instincts of the various personality types, namely the self-preservation instinct, the social instinct, and the sexual instinct. These can bring out different aspects of your personality, also depending on various situations.

Self-Preservation Subtype

The self-preservation subtype focuses mainly on personal well-being. If you have this subtype, you'll mainly be concerned with having your own needs met. You want to be comfortable and secure in your environment, and your behavior will be practical and focused on your own well-being. This can include financial stability in a secure environment.

Those with the self-preservation subtype will usually look for partners who make them feel secure and can contribute to providing a stable environment. They value reliability and dependability. This subtype is good at setting boundaries, establishing stable routines, and avoiding disruptions.

The strength of this subtype is planning, organizing, and taking care of the practical details. However, they can worry excessively about threats and disruptions. They could also struggle to deal with change, as it threatens their sense of stability. They need to become more flexible to adapt to changed circumstances.

Part of their personal growth journey would be to get out of their comfort zones and accept change. They need to develop trust in their own ability to deal with challenges. Balancing their need for security and stability will help them navigate their lives with greater resilience and fulfillment.

Social Subtype

Group identity, belonging, and connecting with others are important to people who have the social subtype. They want to build and maintain relationships and make a positive impact on a larger scale. This subtype usually needs plenty of validation from others, and they have a natural ability to connect with people.

Social subtypes usually look for a partner who shares their values and their passion for making a difference in the world. They want relationships with a shared sense of purpose.

The social subtype can also face challenges like a fear of rejection and being people pleasers. They can also struggle with setting boundaries and prioritizing their own needs. They also need to find a balance between being social and self-care to ensure they have enough energy to pursue their goals.

The personal growth goals for this type should be to explore their own needs and desires outside of community involvement. They need to realize that it's also important to nurture their own goals and aspirations.

Sexual Subtype

The sexual subtype, or one-to-one or intimate subtype, wants intense and passionate relationships with others. They want intense emotional relationships that have emotional depth.

Sexual subtypes usually want partners who share their intensity and desire for intimacy. They want a deep connection with their partner and will prioritize the exploration of shared passions.

This subtype is vulnerable and authentic, which helps them when it comes to forming emotional bonds. Their focus on passion and connection can be exciting and fulfilling in relationships.

The sexual subtype can experience challenges such as being overly focused on their relationships, which can lead to possessiveness or jealousy. They could struggle to set boundaries and to find a balance between their desire for connection, on the one hand, and for self-care and individuality on the other hand.

Sexual subtypes also need to focus on developing their self-worth and an individual sense of identity.

By understanding and embracing their need for intimacy, passion, and vulnerability, people with this subtype can establish intense, meaningful relationships.

Levels of Development, or Health Within the Enneagram Type

The nine development levels of the Enneagram are also called the levels of health. They can be divided into Healthy (levels 1–3), Average (levels 4–6), and Unhealthy (levels 7–9).

The Enneagram also describes a range of levels of health within each type. These levels reflect the degree of self-awareness, personal growth, and psychological well-being that an individual experiences within their type. The levels of health, often depicted on a scale from 1–9, provide a framework to assess the overall functioning of a person within their Enneagram type.

Healthy Levels (Levels 1–3)

At healthy levels, people are self-aware, they have emotional balance, and they're able to manage their behavior.

Average Levels (Levels 4–6)

If you're on the average level, you'll have a mix of healthy and unhealthy characteristics. These people could have unconscious fears and behaviors that could lead to less constructive behavior. At this level, people could struggle with self-regulation.

Unhealthy Levels (Levels 7–9)

If you're at an unhealthy level, you can experience significant distress and emotional imbalance, and your behavior won't be constructive. People on this level can become trapped in repetitive, self-defeating patterns and exhibit extreme versions of their type's negative traits. The lower levels often involve severe emotional and psychological challenges.

How to Gain Self-Awareness by Using the Enneagram

The Enneagram can help you with gaining self-awareness, and you can use it as a tool for personal growth.

It can be useful in helping you uncover your unconscious patterns of thinking, feeling, and behaving. Learning more about your Enneagram type can also help you gain a deeper understanding of motivations, needs, fears, and desires.

You will begin to recognize patterns that could be limiting your growth, and you'll be able to navigate your life with a better understanding of yourself.

Each Enneagram type has its own strengths and weaknesses. It teaches you about your strengths and challenges you could face, such as tendencies toward perfectionism, or people pleasing. Once you have this knowledge, you can work on developing your strengths and addressing your weaknesses.

The Enneagram encourages empathy and compassion by highlighting that people can see and experience the world in different ways. It can help us deal with conflicts and communicate more effectively by acknowledging and respecting the unique qualities of others.

Self-discovery and self-awareness can encourage our personal growth and transformation. When we become aware of our unconscious patterns, habits, and tendencies, we can choose to break free from limiting patterns and develop healthier ways of being.

It's not about boxing yourself into a particular personality type. Instead, it aims to help people integrate all aspects of themselves, both positive and challenging. By embracing our strengths and addressing our blind spots, we can strive toward wholeness and authenticity. We can also work on expressing ourselves in more authentic ways.

Using the Enneagram to Gain Self-Awareness—Jean's Story

Jean was on a journey of self-discovery and wanted to make improvements to her life and grow as a person. She had heard that the Enneagram could help her gain a better understanding of herself.

Jean was excited and eager to learn more about the Enneagram. She discovered that this system divided people into nine different personality types, each with unique patterns of thinking, feeling, and behaving.

Jean decided to do a quiz to discover her Enneagram type. She answered a series of questions and was excited to discover that she was a Type 2, or Helper, on the Enneagram. This type is generous, caring, and enjoys helping others. Jean felt that her values aligned with that of Type 2.

Jean came to realize that she could also use the Enneagram to gain more self-awareness and to grow as a person. The Enneagram made her realize what the strengths and weaknesses of her personality type were, and she also developed a better understanding of her behavioral patterns.

Jean realized that she had a deep desire to be needed by others, which caused her to neglect her own needs. She began to see that her need to gain validation from others was influencing how she was making decisions. Following the Enneagram gave her more insight into why she was acting the way she was. She started to challenge her habitual ways of thinking and behaving and started to make an effort to break free from certain tendencies. She realized she couldn't spend her entire life pleasing others and doing things because other people wanted her to do them in a certain way.

She began paying more attention to her self-care and setting boundaries in her relationships. Jean asked for help from others instead of always being the one who offered it. She also started working on validating herself and not always looking for approval from others.

Jean became more self-aware and that helped her to make more conscious choices and live a more fulfilling life. She also began to realize that personal growth and discovering more about herself would be a lifelong journey. The Enneagram became her compass in life, and it guided her to greater self-acceptance and a deeper connection to herself, and others.

Practical Journal Activity: Determine Your Enneagram Type

Put aside some quiet time for self-reflection and write down your thoughts and responses in your notebook or journal. You could also use any of your electronic devices.

Read through the descriptions of the nine Enneagram types earlier in the chapter. While you're reading, decide which of the descriptions you can relate to the most.

It's important to keep in mind that you will have characteristics from various types. You should try to identify one that is the most dominant for you. That will be your core Enneagram type. Also keep the wings and subtypes in mind.

Reflection

Consider the following questions while you do reflection:

- Which of the types resonates the most with your desires and core motivations?
- Which type aligns with your behavior and core fears?
- How does the dominant type align with your strengths and weaknesses?

Activities

- After you've read all the descriptions, choose the top three types that you can relate to.
- Consider the core behaviors, fears, and motivations of the three types and decide how they align with your tendencies and experiences.
- After you've done this, rank the types according to how well they represent your dominant traits.

Remember that this self-assessment is only a starting point for further exploration. You can take formal Enneagram assessments or work with a qualified Enneagram practitioner for a more comprehensive understanding of your type.

Key Takeaways

- The Enneagram has a long history that can be traced back to ancient times.

- Oscar Ichazo developed the modern Enneagram by focusing on the psychological aspects and linking them to certain types of behavior.

- Each of the nine types represents a different way of feeling, thinking, and behaving.

- The first Enneagram type is the Perfectionist/Reformer, who is rational and strives for perfection. They want to improve themselves and those around them.

- Reformers need to realize that they can't save everyone, and they need to make time for themselves.

- The Helper/Giver is the second Enneagram type. They want to be loved and appreciated.

- Helpers need to take care of themselves so that they don't get overwhelmed by the needs of others.

- Enneagram Type 3 is the Achiever/Performer. The Achiever wants to be successful and to be admired.

- Achievers should try to be more authentic and take breaks to reconnect with themselves.

- The Individualist/Romantic is Enneagram Type 4. Individualists want to establish their own meaningful lives.

- Individualists should accept that they aren't their feelings. Their feelings are just telling them something about themselves in the present moment.

- The Investigator/Observer is Type 5 on the Enneagram. They are analytical people who want to obtain more knowledge about the world.

- Investigators should try not to live too much in their minds.

- Loyalists/Skeptic, the sixth of the Enneagram types, are committed and responsible people. They value trust and reliability.

- Loyalists should deal with their stress via healthy coping mechanisms.

- The Enthusiast/Epicure, or Type 7, is adventurous and usually looks for stimulation.

- Enthusiasts need to learn to listen to other people.

- The Challenger/Protector is Type 8 on the Enneagram. They are strong-willed, confident people.

- The Challenger should learn to act with self-restraint.

- Peacemakers/Mediator, the ninth Enneagram type, are easygoing and avoid conflict.

- Peacemakers need to realize their needs and desires are also important.

- Enneagram types can also be understood through their wings, subtypes, and levels of health.

- Enneagram wings are the influences other Enneagram types, which are located on the different sides of your core personality, can have on the dominant type. The Enneagram wings can enhance or diminish your core traits.

- Subtypes are three different instincts of the various personality types. These subtypes are self-preservation, social, and sexual.

- The Enneagram has nine development levels which are also called levels of health.

- The levels of health provide a framework to assess the overall functioning of a person within their Enneagram type.

- The Enneagram can be used to gain self-awareness as a tool for personal growth.

Chapter 2:

The System for Understanding Personality Types for Better Relationships

The Enneagram is primarily rooted in psychology, spirituality, and ancient wisdom traditions rather than neurobiology.

While the Enneagram can be a helpful tool, it's important to keep in mind that it's not meant for official diagnosis. Its insights into personality are based on observations and interpretations of human behavior and not extensive research and validation, compared to some other established personality tools. It does, therefore, not have the same level of evidence supporting its claims.

Following the Enneagram types too strictly can lead to overgeneralization, as it puts people into very distinct types. It's important to take into consideration that people are multifaceted, and that they could exhibit behavior and traits that don't fit into specific Enneagram types.

It's important to appreciate both the benefits and limitations of the Enneagram.

Overview of the Psychological Theory of the Enneagram

The Enneagram is a powerful tool for personal growth and self-discovery, offering insights into our core fears, motivations, and patterns of behavior. By working with the Enneagram, we can increase our self-awareness and facilitate positive change in our lives.

The Enneagram can be used in various ways for personal growth.

It helps us uncover our fears and desires, shedding light on what drives our thoughts, emotions, and actions. Through self-reflection and exploration, we can identify the core fear that underlies our behavior, such as fear of abandonment, failure, or being unloved. Understanding these fears enables us to gain insight into how they shape our lives and relationships.

The Enneagram exposes the patterns and defense mechanisms that each personality type employs to cope with their core fears. By becoming aware of these patterns, we can recognize when we are operating on autopilot and engaging in unhealthy behaviors. This awareness empowers us to interrupt negative cycles, challenge self-limiting beliefs, and make conscious choices aligned with our personal growth goals.

The Enneagram can be a mirror for our strengths, weaknesses, and blind spots. Through self-observation and mindfulness, we can cultivate a deeper understanding of our thoughts, emotions, and actions. This heightened self-awareness allows us to catch ourselves in the midst of automatic reactions, pause, and choose more constructive responses. It also opens up opportunities for personal growth by helping us identify areas where we may be stuck or resistant to change.

Each Enneagram type has a growth path associated with it. Understanding the specific areas of development and potential challenges for our type can guide us in our personal growth journey. By focusing on these areas and intentionally working on them, we can break free from self-imposed limitations and expand our capacities. Embracing growth opportunities and leveraging our unique strengths fosters personal transformation and supports us in becoming the best version of ourselves.

The Enneagram teaches us to develop compassion, both for ourselves and others. As we gain insight into our own fears and motivations, we become more understanding and empathetic toward the struggles and perspectives of others. This empathy enhances our relationships and fosters a greater sense of connection and harmony.

The Enneagram can also help us when it comes to conflict resolution. If we have awareness of what triggers others, we can treat them with more empathy and find constructive ways to address the needs of everyone involved.

Knowing the Enneagram can help us appreciate human diversity. It focuses on the unique strengths, contributions, and perspectives of every person. If we can appreciate and value these differences, we can create an inclusive environment where everyone's talents are recognized.

How the Enneagram Helped Me Develop More Compassion with Others

I am a Type 1 on the Enneagram, or the Perfectionist. I want to do things in what I see as the right way, and I can be critical of myself, and of others, when it comes to mistakes.

As I advanced through life, I started to realize it would probably benefit my personal and business relationships if I could learn how to have more empathy or compassion for others. This didn't come that naturally to me because, not only was I a perfectionist, but I was also ambitious.

The Enneagram helped me to develop empathy in the following ways:

- It has helped me start to understand my own need for perfectionism better, and how it can affect my interactions with others. It has helped me see that others have their own challenges, and I need to treat them with empathy.

- It has also helped me realize I have a strong inner critic that is driving me to judge myself and that also has an impact on my relationships. It has encouraged me to start practicing self-compassion and ignoring this inner critic.

- It has also helped me to appreciate different perspectives and be more open to doing things in different ways. I have started to realize that there's more than one valid way to approach life and interact with others.

How the Enneagram Can Help People Recognize and Overcome Their Obstacles

The Enneagram is a valuable tool for individuals to recognize and overcome their personal obstacles by providing insights into their patterns of thinking, feeling, and behaving.

By identifying their Enneagram type, individuals gain awareness of their habitual patterns and tendencies that may be hindering their personal growth. This self-awareness is essential for recognizing and understanding personal obstacles.

The Enneagram can also help people identify their limiting beliefs and behaviors, which could be holding them back from reaching their potential. If people are able to recognize these patterns, it makes it easier for them to challenge these beliefs and reframe them in a more positive way.

Each Enneagram type has specific defense mechanisms that they use to protect themselves from personal pain. These types of mechanisms can become obstacles to personal growth. If people understand their own defense mechanisms, they can choose healthier ways to react in different situations.

The Enneagram recognizes that people have qualities and strengths from different Enneagram types on top of their core type. By integrating and embodying healthy aspects of other types, people can then broaden their perspectives and overcome the limitations of their core type. The integration process encourages personal growth and helps us to overcome obstacles by changing our behaviors.

The Enneagram also encourages compassionate self-acceptance and resilience. People are taught to approach their challenges and weaknesses with acceptance and self-compassion. People can approach their flaws without judging themselves by understanding that their Enneagram type is a framework, and it's not their fixed identity.

Engaging with a supportive community that shares knowledge of the Enneagram can provide people with support and guidance in overcoming personal obstacles. It's useful to connect with others with similar experiences and to learn from their journeys.

Growth Paths for the Different Enneagram Types

The Enneagram can help the different types understand their growth paths.

Type 1—The Perfectionist/Reformer

Perfectionists need to accept themselves and that they're imperfect beings. It's important for Perfectionists to learn to balance their need for perfection with compassion for themselves, as well as flexibility and adaptability.

The rigid need for perfection can make someone more susceptible to mental health issues. To become resilient, and build on this, one needs to have a more flexible approach to life. If you're more resilient, you're better able to bounce back when you have to deal with adversity and setbacks in your life. People with a flexible approach to life usually deal with challenges more effectively. If they become more open-minded, they can also lead more spontaneous and creative lives.

Developing emotional intelligence is another important aspect of the Perfectionist's growth path. They tend to suppress or try to ignore their emotions. It's important for them to learn to show their vulnerability to others and obtain support from the people who are important to them in their lives.

Ultimately, Perfectionists need to find a healthy balance between their need to constantly improve and their acceptance that they are far from perfect, and that this is normal.

Type 2—The Helper/Giver

The Helper needs to establish healthy boundaries in their relationships and recognize their own needs. Helpers need to learn that they are worthy as themselves, not only when they're helping others. They are as deserving of love and care as anyone else.

These types of people are naturally caring, selfless, and supportive of others. They can find it fulfilling to be needed and appreciated, but this can cause them to neglect their own well-being, and they can become dependent on this type of validation.

When Helpers start to work on their growth, they need to prioritize their self-care. They need to learn to fulfill their needs and desires without relying on others.

Helpers need to establish boundaries in relationships so that they're not constantly prioritizing the needs of others above their own. They need to learn how to say no and to set limits.

Prioritizing their own needs will also help them develop a deeper sense of self-awareness and a better understanding of their own emotions.

Helpers can be hard on themselves and may feel guilty or selfish when they prioritize their own needs. By offering themselves the same kindness and understanding they usually give others, Helpers need to develop a healthier and more balanced perspective on self-care.

Helpers should also explore activities and hobbies that they enjoy. This can help them lead fulfilling and meaningful lives.

In the end, growth for Helpers is about finding a balance between caring for others and for themselves. This will help them experience greater personal fulfillment and stronger relationships with others.

Type 3—The Achiever/Performer

Achievers need to shift their focus from external validation to self-acceptance and inner fulfillment. They need to connect with their authentic selves and prioritize their personal values over what society expects from them. This means they need to connect with their inner motivations and align their actions with their sense of purpose. It's only possible to achieve real growth if you lead an authentic life, and not according to what other people expect from you. For example, you shouldn't be following a career your parents want you to or get married to someone who your parents think is a good option.

The Achiever needs to learn to live their own life and to shift their focus from wanting external validation from others to self-acceptance and inner fulfillment. Achievers usually have a strong drive to succeed, and they are good at setting goals and achieving them. However, this can cause them to rely too much on external achievements to give them a sense of self-worth.

They normally tend to be overly critical of themselves and need to be kinder to themselves. If they can learn to accept their faults, they can develop a healthier self-image.

Achievers also need to learn to be more present in the moment and to appreciate their journey through life rather than just focusing on the destination.

Developing authentic relationships is essential for Achievers' growth. By fostering genuine connections based on authenticity and mutual support, Achievers will experience a sense of acceptance and deeper fulfillment.

Type 4—The Individualist/Romantic

The Individualist needs to work on their self-esteem. They often feel misunderstood and different from others. Their self-worth is often dependent on the external validation of their abilities, and they need to realize that they're inherently valuable as human beings.

They also need to stop comparing themselves to others and accept themselves for who they are. They need to embrace being vulnerable without judging themselves, and they should treat themselves with the same kindness with which they treat others.

Individualists need to attempt not to be overwhelmed by their inner world. Mindfulness and creative outlets can help them find stability and balance.

They also need to try to find meaning in everyday life, and they must realize that simple joys can make them feel content. They don't always have to look for extraordinary experiences.

Individualists will also benefit from forming relationships with others who understand them and appreciate their individuality.

Type 5—The Investigator/Observer

Investigators need to overcome the tendency to withdraw and should work at forming meaningful relationships, which will also help them develop a deeper understanding of themselves.

The Investigator needs to develop emotional intelligence so that they can engage more fully and authentically with the world. They tend to rely on their intellect and become detached from their emotions.

Investigators tend to withdraw from excessive social interaction and conserve their energy by observing and analyzing their surroundings. They need to challenge their tendency to retreat and make an effort to participate in social interactions.

The Investigator should share their knowledge with others. They could fear being overwhelmed and drained if they do this. However, sharing their expertise can help them create stronger relationships with others and it can contribute to their growth.

The Investigator needs to find a balance between gathering knowledge and using it in their lives. If they focus too much on collecting information and analyzing it, it could hold them back from taking action. Investigators need to empower themselves by putting their knowledge into practice.

Investigators also need to challenge their tendency to isolate themselves and retreat into their minds. They could try to create an emotional distance between themselves and others as a form of self-preservation.

If Investigators achieve their goal of growth, they'll be able to engage more fully with the world, and build better connections with others.

Type 6—The Loyalist/Skeptic

Loyalists are characterized by their desire for security and their tendency to anticipate and prepare for potential threats and dangers.

The growth path for a Loyalist involves a journey toward self-confidence, inner strength, and a balanced approach to fear and anxiety.

The first step toward growth for a Loyalist is developing self-awareness. This involves recognizing and acknowledging their fears, anxieties, and the underlying motivations that drive their behavior. By understanding the patterns and triggers that contribute to their anxiety, Loyalists can begin to take conscious control of their reactions.

Loyalists tend to look for external sources of security and rely heavily on others for guidance and reassurance. Their growth path involves developing trust in their own judgment and cultivating a connection with their inner guidance. This can be achieved through practices such as meditation, self-reflection, and listening to their intuition.

Loyalists often struggle with uncertainty and the fear of the unknown. The growth path involves learning to embrace uncertainty and developing a greater tolerance for ambiguity. This can be done by gradually exposing themselves to situations that challenge their need for certainty and actively reframing their perspective on uncertainty as an opportunity for growth and learning.

Building self-confidence is a crucial aspect of growth for Loyalists. This involves recognizing their strengths, talents, and abilities, and acknowledging their past accomplishments. By focusing on their capabilities and nurturing their self-esteem, Loyalists can gradually let go of excessive doubt and become more self-assured.

Loyalists have a strong sense of loyalty toward others, often seeking validation and support from external sources. However, to foster growth, it's important for Loyalists to balance their loyalty with a sense of autonomy and self-reliance. This means developing healthy boundaries, asserting their needs, and making decisions based on their own values and beliefs rather than solely relying on others' opinions.

Courage is a key virtue for Loyalists to develop on their growth path. This involves facing their fears, stepping out of their comfort zones, and taking calculated risks. By gradually exposing themselves to their anxieties and challenging their self-imposed limitations, Loyalists can expand their comfort zone and develop greater resilience.

Overall, the growth path for a Loyalist involves developing self-awareness, cultivating trust in themselves, embracing uncertainty, building self-confidence, balancing loyalty and autonomy, as well as cultivating courage. By actively engaging in this growth journey, Loyalists can transform their anxieties into strengths, and experience a more balanced and fulfilling life.

Type 7—The Enthusiast/Epicure

Type 7 individuals are characterized by their desire for joy and variety and their avoidance of pain or discomfort.

The growth path for an Enthusiast involves a journey toward self-awareness, balance, and a deeper connection with their inner selves.

The first step toward growth for an Enthusiast is developing self-reflection and self-awareness. This involves taking the time to understand their motivations, fears, and desires. By examining their patterns of thinking, feeling, and behaving, Enthusiasts can gain insight into their tendencies to avoid pain and seek constant stimulation and pleasure.

Enthusiasts often have a strong aversion to discomfort, pain, and negative emotions. The growth path involves learning to embrace and face these challenging emotions and experiences. By allowing themselves to fully experience and process uncomfortable feelings, Enthusiasts can develop emotional resilience and a greater capacity for self-discovery and growth.

Enthusiasts tend to have a restless and future-oriented mindset, always seeking the next exciting experience. The growth path involves cultivating mindfulness and learning to be present in the current moment. Mindfulness practices such as meditation, deep breathing, or body awareness exercises can help Enthusiasts ground themselves in the present and cultivate a sense of inner calm and contentment.

Enthusiasts often struggle with commitment and can easily get distracted by new opportunities and experiences. The growth path involves developing the ability to commit and follow through on chosen paths or projects. By focusing their energy and attention on their goals, Enthusiasts can develop a sense of accomplishment and fulfillment.

Enthusiasts have a tendency to stay on the surface and avoid deeper emotional exploration. The growth path involves venturing into their inner depths and exploring their deeper emotions, fears, and insecurities. This can be done through journaling, therapy, or engaging in meaningful conversations with trusted individuals. By acknowledging and integrating their shadows, Enthusiasts can experience greater self-acceptance and wholeness.

Enthusiasts have a natural inclination toward excess and overindulgence. The growth path involves finding balance and moderation in their pursuit of pleasure and stimulation. This means learning to discern genuine needs from momentary desires and practicing self-control and restraint when necessary. By finding a healthy balance, Enthusiasts can avoid burnout, and they can also lead more satisfying lives.

Enthusiasts can fear being still and quiet, as it can bring up uncomfortable emotions or a sense of missing out. The growth path involves intentionally seeking moments of stillness and silence. Through practices such as meditation, nature walks, or reflective activities, Enthusiasts can connect with their inner stillness and develop a sense of inner peace and contentment.

By taking part in this growth journey, Enthusiasts can cultivate self-awareness, embrace discomfort, and can lead more joyful and fulfilling lives.

Type 8—The Challenger/Protector

Challengers are characterized by their desire for control, assertiveness, and protection of themselves and others.

The growth path for a Challenger involves a journey toward self-awareness, vulnerability, and healthy expression of power.

The first step toward growth for a Challenger is developing self-reflection and self-awareness. This involves examining their motivations, fears, and patterns of behavior. By gaining insight into their tendencies to control or dominate others, Challengers can better understand the impact of their actions and develop a more conscious approach to their interactions.

Challengers often fear vulnerability and have a tendency to protect themselves by being strong and independent. The growth path involves embracing vulnerability and recognizing that it is not a sign of weakness but a pathway to deeper connections and personal growth. By allowing themselves to be vulnerable, Challengers can cultivate more authentic relationships and open themselves up to support and understanding from others.

Challengers have a strong desire to protect and support others. The growth path involves developing empathy and compassion toward the needs and experiences of others. By recognizing and valuing the perspectives and emotions of those around them, Challengers can create healthier dynamics in their relationships and foster a more inclusive and supportive environment.

Challengers have a natural inclination toward asserting power and control. The growth path involves finding a healthy balance in the expression of power and recognizing when to soften or relinquish control. This means understanding that true strength lies not only in dominating others but also in empowering and collaborating with them. By embracing collaboration and shared power, Challengers can foster more balanced and harmonious relationships.

Challengers often have a tendency to suppress or dismiss their own emotions. The growth path involves developing emotional intelligence and self-regulation skills. This includes becoming more attuned to their own feelings, expressing emotions in a healthy way, and being open to receiving and processing feedback. By embracing emotional vulnerability and practicing self-awareness, Challengers can build more authentic and fulfilling connections with others.

Challengers have a strong sense of discernment and a desire for justice. The growth path involves channeling their assertiveness in a constructive and compassionate manner. By developing discernment grounded in empathy and fairness, Challengers can advocate for themselves and others with integrity and consideration for the well-being of all involved.

By actively engaging in this growth journey, Challengers can cultivate self-awareness, embrace vulnerability, balance power and control, develop empathy and emotional intelligence, and create more harmonious and fulfilling relationships in their lives.

Type 9—The Peacemaker/Mediator

Peacemakers are characterized by their desire for inner peace, harmony, and avoidance of conflict.

The growth path for a Peacemaker involves a journey toward self-awareness, assertiveness, and embracing personal desires and needs.

The first step toward growth for a Peacemaker is developing self-reflection and self-awareness. This involves examining their motivations, fears, and patterns of behavior. By gaining insight into their tendencies to avoid conflict or merge with others' desires, Peacemakers can begin to understand the ways in which they may have neglected their own needs and wants.

Peacemakers often struggle with asserting themselves and expressing their opinions and desires. The growth path involves learning to embrace assertiveness and speaking up for themselves. This means recognizing that their voice and perspective are valuable and deserve to be shared. By actively asserting themselves in a healthy and respectful manner, Peacemakers can establish boundaries, advocate for their needs, and create more balanced relationships.

Peacemakers have a tendency to merge with the desires and agendas of others, often losing touch with their own passions and aspirations. The growth path involves identifying and pursuing their own personal desires. This means taking the time to explore their own interests, dreams, and goals, and giving themselves permission to prioritize their own needs and aspirations. By reconnecting with their own desires, Peacemakers can cultivate a greater sense of purpose and fulfillment.

Peacemakers tend to avoid conflict and often prioritize maintaining harmony in their relationships. The growth path involves learning to engage constructively with conflict. This includes recognizing that healthy conflict can lead to growth and resolution and actively participating in discussions and negotiations. By developing conflict resolution skills and expressing their needs and opinions honestly, Peacemakers can contribute to more authentic and balanced relationships.

Peacemakers often prioritize the needs of others over their own, neglecting self-care and self-expression. The growth path involves prioritizing self-care and finding healthy outlets for self-expression. This may involve engaging in activities that bring joy and fulfillment, practicing self-care rituals, and exploring creative or artistic pursuits. By nurturing their own well-being and expressing themselves authentically, Peacemakers can enhance their sense of self and overall satisfaction in life.

Peacemakers may struggle with a lack of motivation or difficulty initiating action. The growth path involves cultivating inner drive and motivation. This includes identifying personal values, setting goals, and developing a sense of purpose. By connecting with their inner passions and aspirations, Peacemakers can find the energy and motivation to take meaningful action in their lives.

By actively engaging in this growth journey, Peacemakers can cultivate self-awareness, embrace assertiveness, prioritize personal desires and needs, engage constructively with conflict, practice self-care and self-expression, cultivate inner drive and motivation, and find a greater sense of fulfillment and authenticity in their lives.

The Enneagram Encourages Personal Challenges—Mia's Story

Mia is a Type 7 on the Enneagram. She struggled with commitment and often found that she was distracted by new experiences. The Enneagram has helped her to overcome some of the challenges in her life and to achieve more.

Mia had an insatiable curiosity and she enjoyed starting new projects and hobbies. However, she often didn't follow through on things and gave up on her hobbies as soon as she started them. This became a serious frustration to her, as she felt as if she wasn't achieving anything, and she ended up with many half-finished paintings, unfinished novels, and many regrets about wasted time.

Mia jumped between projects, and she was always excited about starting new things. This did bring her some joy, but she also still felt as if she wasn't fulfilling her potential.

Mia was committed to her own personal growth, and she started doing research on how she could deal with the challenges in her life. She discovered the Enneagram system and felt that it would give her more insight into her personality type.

While studying the Enneagram, she came to the conclusion that her type got easily distracted, and a struggle to commit was also part of her personality.

Driven by a desire for growth and a sense of accomplishment, Mia decided to improve herself by learning more about her characteristics through using the Enneagram. She also got a mentor who specialized in Enneagram coaching and who helped her to channel her enthusiasm and focus her energy effectively.

Together, they explored the Enthusiast's growth path. Mia discovered that by becoming aware of her patterns and tendencies, she could take steps toward developing commitment and follow-through on her chosen paths.

She set goals for herself, which involved selecting a few projects or interests that truly resonated with her deepest desires and values. Instead of scattering her energy in multiple directions, she concentrated her efforts on a select few, which helped her focus on how she was investing her time, dedication, and perseverance into each project.

Whenever Mia felt there were new opportunities that she wanted to explore, she would pause and first consider what she really wanted to do and how many other responsibilities she already had. She had acknowledged to herself that she had taken on too much in the past, such as registering for different study courses, and then not completing all of them.

She reminded herself that she would feel a greater sense of accomplishment if she stuck with something and completed it, rather than ending up with a lot of unfinished courses and projects. By consciously redirecting her attention and focusing on her goals, Mia started to feel more satisfied and as if she was achieving her purpose.

As time passed, Mia's commitment and follow-through improved. She completed projects that she once thought were beyond her reach. She also finished study courses for which she had registered in the past and continued her studies after achieving these qualifications. Her dedication and perseverance paid off, and she started to reap the rewards of her focused efforts.

She discovered a sense of inner fulfillment and a deep sense of accomplishment that came from seeing her projects through to completion. She realized that commitment was not about limiting herself but rather about channeling her enthusiasm and focus in a way that allowed her to grow and achieve a lasting impact.

Mia's transformation inspired her family and friends, and some of them who previously struggled to focus and complete projects also made progress in this regard.

Through her journey with the Enneagram, Mia learned commitment and follow-through. She learned to channel her enthusiasm effectively.

Practical Exercise—Explore Your Enneagram Type

The following exercises and journal prompts can help you delve deeper into your Enneagram type and find your personal growth path.

- Think about the desires, needs, and fears that might be influencing your thoughts, feelings, and actions. Write about this in your journal. How does this become evident in different areas of your life?

- Consider situations, challenges, and relationships that seem to repeat in your life. Are there recurring patterns and themes? In your journal, write about how these recurring patterns or themes (if there are any) relate to your Enneagram type. Will they impact your growth or well-being?

- Reflect on how your early childhood could have influenced your Enneagram type. Think about significant events that you experienced as a child, family dynamics, or cultural influences that could have influenced your development. Write about these key influences that could have influenced your Enneagram type. How could these experiences affect your behavior, beliefs, and patterns of thinking?

- Think about how your Enneagram type manifests during times of severe stress. How do your behaviors, thoughts, and emotions change during times of stress? Do you experience any unhealthy behaviors and thought patterns during times of stress?

- Consider the fears and desires that are associated with your Enneagram type. How do these fears and desires influence your choices, relationships, and personal development? In your journal, write about how your fears and desires influenced you. How can you work with them to facilitate personal growth?

- Set aside time every day to observe your thoughts, feelings, and behavior. In your journal, write about what you've noticed about yourself during your period of self-observation. How can you use self-awareness to make conscious changes that align with your personal growth?

- You should also ask your family members or friends who are familiar with the Enneagram for feedback. What have they observed about

69

your Enneagram type and growth type? These perspectives can be valuable in helping you understand more about yourself.

Key Takeaways

- The Enneagram's insight into personality is based on observations of human behavior, fears, desires, and motivations.

- We can increase our self-awareness and facilitate positive change by working with the Enneagram.

- The Enneagram could help you uncover your fears and desires through self-reflection and exploration.

- The Enneagram also exposes the patterns and defense mechanisms the different personality types use to cope with their fears.

- There is a growth path associated with each Enneagram type. Embracing the growth opportunities can help us become the best versions of ourselves.

- The Enneagram can help with conflict resolution.

- The Enneagram can also help us appreciate human diversity.

- There are different growth paths for the different Enneagram types.

Chapter 3:

Identify Your Personality Type

Learning more about the Enneagram has been a transformative life experience for many people. Bestselling author and speaker, Brené Brown, has mentioned the significant role the Enneagram played in her personal development journey.

Brown has said that she appreciates how the Enneagram can help people understand the different ways they themselves and the people around them interact with the world. She has also written the foreword for the book *The Enneagram of Belonging* by Chris Heuertz (Rush to Press, 2020).

In the foreword, she shares how his first book, *The Sacred Enneagram,* affected her and states that the author's work has changed the way she sees the world and the people around her. It has also helped her to make peace with her vulnerabilities and imperfections.

Brown's acknowledgment of the significance of the Enneagram proves its potential as a useful tool for personal growth.

The fact is, the Enneagram can help us communicate better by understanding how our own personality type, and the types of the people in our lives, communicate. If we know our own Enneagram type and understand how it communicates, we can express ourselves more clearly.

The Enneagram can help us connect better to others by reducing misunderstandings and building empathetic relationships that are based on respect.

Using the Enneagram to Determine Your Personality Type

When you're going to use the Enneagram to determine your personality type, you first need to familiarize yourself with the system. You need to understand the core types and how they all have distinct patterns of behavior, thinking, and feeling. This will involve studying the descriptions and profiles of the different types.

Self-reflection can help you when it comes to identifying your type. Introspection can help you analyze your thoughts, emotions, and behavior. It will be easier to recognize the patterns and tendencies that define you.

Getting feedback from the different people in your life can give you more insight into your Enneagram type. Professionals who understand the Enneagram can also help us gain an objective view of our personality traits and tendencies. Their insights and observations can help us narrow down our Enneagram type.

Enneagram assessments can serve as useful tools in helping us identify our personality types. These tests can usually be completed online and most often consist of a series of questions designed to evaluate our tendencies and preferences. You need to approach these assessments with an open mind and regard them as a supplemental resource to determining your Enneagram type.

How Childhood Memories and Experiences Can Affect Your Enneagram Type

Childhood patterns can also help us understand our Enneagram type. Early experiences can shape personality development, and our coping and defense mechanisms can align with specific Enneagram types.

Exploring childhood memories and experiences is important because our earliest years can play a crucial role in shaping who we become as people. Childhood experiences and relationships can make lasting impressions on our developing minds and lay the foundations for our beliefs, behaviors, and emotional patterns.

During childhood, our brains absorb information and experiences like sponges. Our interactions with childhood caregivers, family members, and the environment around us have a strong influence on our sense of self, attachment styles, and the development of our personality.

Discovering your childhood memories can give you the following understanding of your personality type:

- Your beliefs about yourself, others, and the world around you are usually influenced by childhood experiences. When we examine these early experiences, we can uncover the beliefs that formed our personality patterns. For example, you could be inclined to be a Type 2, or Helper, on the Enneagram. You should then consider if your mother or other caretakers may have modeled this behavior when you were a child.

- Your attachment style, which determines how you form relationships in adulthood, is usually established in early childhood. Our relationships with our early caregivers influence how we relate to others and how we deal with intimacy and fears of abandonment. Understanding our early attachment experiences can help us understand our later relationships and identify where we need to grow.

- Your childhood experiences can also influence how you develop emotional regulation skills. The way in which our emotions were acknowledged, expressed, or suppressed during our childhoods can determine our emotional responses as adults. If we reflect on the emotional experiences we had as children, it can help us understand how we learned to cope with and manage our emotions.

- You also learn your coping mechanisms and how to cope with the world during childhood. The behaviors we learn during childhood can become ingrained patterns that last into adulthood. If we understand these patterns, we can see how we should change our unhealthy behaviors and develop better ways of dealing with life's challenges.

- Working through your childhood memories and pain can help you heal past wounds and grow as a person. This process will help us gain self-acceptance and self-compassion, and we can get out of repetitive patterns that no longer work for us in our lives.

How Childhood Trauma Could Have Affected Your Personality Type

If you experience trauma during your childhood, it can continue to affect you as an adult, and it will influence your personality type.

Our relationships with our childhood caretakers and our early experiences shape the way we perceive and interact with the world, and will affect our beliefs, responses, and behaviors as adults.

Aspects of your personality that can be affected by childhood trauma include the following:

- You may struggle to regulate your emotions as an adult, as a result of the trauma you suffered during childhood. It could also be difficult for you to express your emotions.

- You might not trust others, and this could pose a challenge when it comes to establishing secure relationships and attachments. You'll find it difficult to rely on others for support and connection.

- You have developed negative beliefs about yourself, and you feel unworthy. You don't value yourself and your talents.

- You could have developed unhealthy ways to cope with stress. This could include substance abuse, isolating yourself, avoidance, or other self-destructive ways to deal with stress.

- Since you've lived with stress and trauma since early childhood, you could be living in a state of heightened alertness and have become hypervigilant. You could find it difficult to relax or could become chronically anxious.

- You could find it difficult to set healthy boundaries in your relationships and even find yourself becoming enmeshed with others. You could even become avoidant in an effort to protect yourself from further harm.

So, how would childhood trauma, or even childhood memories, affect your Enneagram type?

Firstly, the Enneagram can give you a better understanding of how your past experiences have influenced your current personality type.

For example, Sarah is an Enneagram Type 6, or Loyalist, who had endured a difficult childhood marked by instability and uncertainty. There was constant tension in her home. Her caregivers were unpredictable, and she never really felt safe. These memories left her with deep emotional scars that also influenced the development of her Enneagram personality type.

Sarah was haunted by her memories of neglect during her childhood; she was rarely consoled or given reassurance when she was afraid. The adults in the family were also always fighting around her, and made her feel even more anxious and abandoned, especially when her parents forgot to fetch her from school when they were drunk.

She realized that these traumas had a profound impact on her Enneagram personality type. They shaped her deep-seated fear of the world's unpredictability and her need for security and stability. She started to understand why she was always looking for safety and security in her relationships.

Her experiences continued to influence her behavior and thought patterns as she got older. She developed a keen sense of hypervigilance, always anticipating potential threats or dangers, which was to her benefit in the workplace, even though she felt stressed a lot of the time.

Through her Enneagram journey, Sarah gained insight into the ways her childhood trauma influenced her Type 6 personality. She recognized the roots of her anxiety and fear of being abandoned, which caused her self-doubt and excessive worry. The awareness helped her to deal with her fears and develop healthier coping mechanisms.

Sarah's Enneagram exploration also revealed that she was resilient. Despite her difficult past, Sarah was a strong person, and she became a pillar of support for herself and others, thereby creating a sense of safety and reliability in her own life.

Self-Evaluation Techniques That Can Help You Determine Your Enneagram Type

Self-evaluation techniques can help you identify your Enneagram personality type. Just remember that self-assessment is subjective and can be influenced by various things.

Some of the following techniques can help you in the process:

- Read the descriptions and characteristics of the nine Enneagram types. Make sure that you know each type's core fears, motivations, and patterns of behavior. Think about which of the descriptions resonates with you the most and aligns with your experiences.

- Take online Enneagram assessments, as this can be a good starting point for self-evaluation. While they should be used as a tool rather than definitive proof of your Enneagram type, they can give insight and narrow down the possibilities for you. You should combine self-assessment, reflection, and introspection for a more accurate understanding of your type.

- Pay attention to how you think, feel, and behave in certain situations. How do you respond to stress, challenges, and conflict? Are there recurring themes in your emotions, thoughts, and actions?

- Consider your childhood patterns and early life experiences. How did you cope with challenges and what comforted you? If you understand your childhood experiences, you will get a better idea about the origin of some of your personality patterns, and it's easier to see how they align with certain Enneagram types.

- Journal to help you explore your feelings and thoughts. Keep a journal in which you write as often as possible about your values, fears, desires, and experiences. Consider areas in which you may need to grow. Journaling can help you become more aware of patterns and insights that can indicate your Enneagram type.

- Ask your family and friends for feedback about your personality. Their perspectives can give you a better understanding of your strengths, weaknesses, and possible Enneagram type.

- It can also help you to take part in Enneagram discussions and workshops. If you interact with others who know more about the Enneagram than you, they can give you valuable insights and perspectives, as well as opportunities to reflect. Getting feedback from others and exchanging information about your experiences can help you understand your own type better.

Examples of How the Enneagram Has Helped People Improve Their Relationships

The Enneagram has helped many people to improve their understanding and empathy in personal and work relationships. For example, Joan and Tom had been married for several years, but they were frequently in conflict because of their different communication styles. When they learned about the Enneagram, they completed a test, and it turned out that Tom is a Type 1, while Joan is a Type 9. This helped them to understand that Tom is more perfectionistic, while Joan is easygoing and tries to avoid conflict. This enabled them to interact with greater understanding, and they were able to overcome their differences and communicate more effectively.

The Enneagram can also improve work relationships and is useful when it comes to enhancing leadership and team dynamics. One example is Antonio, a Type 3 on the Enneagram who struggled to understand why his team was unmotivated. The Enneagram helped him realize his drive for achievement and being successful at all costs had started to overshadow the needs of his team. He began to adapt his leadership style and gave more recognition to his team members. Overall, he was able to create a more collaborative work environment and improve productivity.

Enneagram Strategies for Dealing with Strained or Difficult Relationships

The Enneagram can be a useful tool for dealing with complicated relationships. You need to understand your own Enneagram type and become aware of your own tendencies and patterns in relationships. Self-awareness also requires you to take responsibility for your own actions, which will make it easier for you to deal with relationship challenges.

It can help to learn more about the Enneagram types of the people who you have difficult relationships with. If you understand what motivates them, you can get insight into their perspectives, which will help you treat them with more empathy.

Every Enneagram type has its own needs and preferences, and you need to respect their boundaries. You need to take their need for personal space, comfort zones, and communication style into consideration.

Compatible Enneagram Types

Enneagram compatibility is complex and depends on the individual dynamics and interactions between people. Compatibility between different people also depends on many different factors in conjunction with the Enneagram.

For example, people need to be able to communicate openly and effectively to be able to understand each other and have a successful relationship. A willingness to empathize and listen to each other also form part of successful communication as a couple.

You also need shared values and beliefs to be compatible as a couple. This will promote a sense of purpose in the relationship.

Couples who are emotionally intelligent fare better when it comes to relationships. They are more empathetic and better able to deal with disagreements and challenges in their relationship. These couples usually have significant self-awareness and good conflict resolution skills.

If couples share the same interests and hobbies, they may be better connected. It can strengthen bonds to take part in activities that are enjoyed by both.

Lifestyle choices and routines can influence compatibility. For example, if you're an introvert who prefers a relaxed, harmonious lifestyle, you might get along better with someone who is the same.

Support networks can also play a role when it comes to the compatibility of relationships. If a couple has supportive friends and family members, the positive environment can enhance their relationship.

Which Enneagram Types Are More Compatible?

The different Enneagram types can actually all have successful relationships with each other. Some of the combinations do, however, have a more natural rapport.

The following Enneagram types could form successful relationships:

- Type 9 (the Peacemaker) and Type 2 (the Helper) are both accommodating people who would prioritize the connection between them and want harmonious relationships. Both types have empathy, and they will support each other and create mutually supportive relationships. Type 9 will appreciate the care and support offered by Type 2, while Type 2 will appreciate the soothing presence of Type 9.

- Type 1 (the Perfectionist) and Type 6 (the Loyalist) are responsible, and they desire security. They are committed to doing what is right, and they stay loyal to their values. Their relationship will be stable, with Type 1 bringing structure and high standards, and Type 6 offering support and loyalty.

85

- Type 3 (the Achiever) and Type 7 (the Enthusiast) are energetic, ambitious, and they enjoy new experiences. These types can inspire and motivate each other to achieve their goals. Type 3 enjoys the adventurous nature of Type 7, while Type 7 will appreciate Type 3's ambitious nature.

- Type 4 (the Individualist) and Type 5 (the Investigator) value introspection, creativity, and intellectual pursuits. They understand each other's need for space and independence. They can support each other when it comes to personal growth and individual expression. Type 4 can offer creativity and emotional insight, while Type 5 will provide intellectual stimulation and a calm presence.

The compatibility of Enneagram types can vary according to the self-awareness and personal growth of the individuals in the relationship.

Which Are the Least Compatible Types?

Certain Enneagram combinations may face more challenges when it comes to relationships.

The following Enneagram types might experience challenges in a relationship:

- Type 1 (the Perfectionist) and Type 8 (the Challenger) have strong personalities and they both want control. While Type 1 wants order and structure, Type 8 wants to challenge authority. They could face power struggles in their relationships since they both want to achieve control.

- Type 3 (the Achiever) and Type 4 (the Individualist) see success in different ways, and they usually have different priorities. Type 3 usually pursues external achievements, and they could struggle to express their emotions. The Type 4 personality is more introspective and wants authentic relationships and strong emotional connections. They could find it difficult to meet each other's needs.

- Type 5 (the Investigator) and Type 7 (the Enthusiast) have different approaches to expending their energy. Type 5 is conservative, enjoys solitude, and conserves their energy. Type 7 is more outgoing and enjoys novelty. Type 5 could find Type 7's high energy levels overwhelming, while Type 7 may see Type 5 as withdrawn and disconnected.

- Type 6 (the Loyalist) and Type 8 (the Challenger) are both strongly focused on self-preservation and are assertive. Their fear responses and motivations are different. The different approaches could lead to power struggles and trust issues.

Compatibility obviously depends on the people involved and how committed they are to understanding each other's needs.

Strategies to Overcome Compatibility Challenges

To overcome the challenges that may arise in any of these pairings, it's essential for individuals to cultivate self-awareness, understanding, and open communication. Here are some strategies that can help each of these pairings overcome their challenges:

Type 1 and Type 8

- Type 1 and Type 8 should listen to each other and aim to understand each other's perspectives and needs.

- They need to realize that communication styles and approaches to authority aren't wrong but that they just express individual preferences.

- These types should work toward finding common ground and sharing goals.

- Type 1 and Type 8 should be consistent and honest in their interactions and behavior.

- They also need to try to understand things from each other's points of view.

Type 3 and Type 4

- Type 3 and Type 4 should value each other's unique strengths and perspectives.

- They need to communicate in an honest way about their expectations, goals, and emotional needs.

- These two types should also find a balance between external achievement and self-expression.

- They should treat each other with compassion and empathy. They should also validate and recognize each other's emotions.

Type 5 and Type 7

- These two types need to communicate openly about their differing needs for solitude and stimulation.

- They need to find a balance between constantly looking for new experiences and allowing each other to have the time and space for introspection and self-care. It's essential that they respect each other's boundaries and need for personal space.

- They need to try to understand each other's approaches to life.

Type 6 and Type 8

- These two types should follow through on the commitments they have made to each other.

- It will also improve their relationship if their communication is open and direct.

- They need to encourage each other's independence and autonomy while also supporting each other.

How People from Different Enneagram Types Overcame Their Challenges

Anna is a Type 2 (the Helper), and Ewan is a Type 5 (the Investigator) on the Enneagram. Anna has a warm and nurturing nature, and she is always ready to help anyone in need. Ewan, on the other hand, prefers keeping to himself and focusing mainly on intellectual pursuits.

Anna and Ewan found themselves working together on a community project to create a neighborhood garden. Their different Enneagram types made it difficult for them to work together at first. Anna was enthusiastic and encouraged connections among the project participants, while Ewan preferred to observe and analyze from a distance. He was feeling overwhelmed by the social interactions.

As they began working side by side, their differences created tension and misunderstandings. Anna felt that Ewan was detached and uninterested, while Ewan found Anna's constant need for social interaction distracting and draining. Both of them became frustrated, and they doubted if they could work together successfully.

The team experienced a major setback when a storm destroyed a big part of the garden they had worked so hard on. Disheartened, the project team struggled to find a way forward. At that moment, Anna's empathetic nature kicked in. She decided to call a meeting to address the challenges they faced.

During the meeting, Ewan quietly observed the group dynamics and listened to the various concerns and suggestions. Inspired by the resilience and determination of his fellow team members, he realized that his analytical skills could contribute to finding practical solutions. Taking a deep breath, he spoke up and shared his ideas on how they could rebuild the garden efficiently with the available resources they had.

He was surprised to find that Anna immediately accepted his suggestions, recognizing the value of his practical insights. She realized that Ewan's reserved demeanor was not a sign of disinterest but rather a reflection of his thoughtful nature. Ewan, in turn, started to appreciate Anna's ability to connect with others and create a sense of community, acknowledging that her warmth and enthusiasm were essential for the project's success.

As they continued to collaborate, Anna and Ewan discovered that their differences were complementary. Anna's nurturing nature made the team feel less anxious, while Ewan's logical thinking helped them to streamline the decision-making process. They learned to use each other's strengths and respect their unique approaches, understanding that compatibility did not mean becoming carbon copies of one another.

Through their shared efforts, the community garden was stronger and more beautiful than ever. The project transformed the neighborhood physically but also fostered a deep sense of connection among the residents. Anna and Ewan realized that their compatibility challenges had ultimately led them to forming a stronger bond and developing a greater appreciation for their individual strengths.

Detailed Description of the Different Enneagram Types

We've looked at the basic characteristics of the different Enneagram types and will now be studying them in more detail.

1. The Perfectionist/Reformer

Perfectionists have a strong desire to live up to their own high standards and strive for perfection in all areas of their lives. They want to improve the world around them and have a strong sense of responsibility.

Characteristics

Perfectionists have a good work ethic, and they pay attention to detail. They have high standards for themselves and others. They are self-disciplined and reliable people who strive for excellence in everything they do.

Fears

They fear making mistakes and feel everything they do must be perfect at all times. They worry about being inadequate or incompetent and don't deal well with criticism.

Desires

The Perfectionist wants to be a good person and live up to their own ideals. They strive to make a positive contribution to the world.

Communication Style

They communicate in a clear and persuasive style. Perfectionists can express themselves in a clear and articulate way. They also expect others to express their thoughts clearly and efficiently.

Strengths

Perfectionists have a strong sense of responsibility and a commitment to doing things right. They are self-motivated, and it's usually easy for them to achieve their goals.

Potential Challenges

Perfectionists can be extremely critical of themselves and everyone around them. They can struggle to accept their own errors and those of others.

Perfectionists can become rigid in their thinking and have difficulty adapting to unexpected changes or situations that do not align with their ideals.

Growth and Development

If Perfectionists want to grow as people, they need to learn to be kind to themselves and to learn that it is normal to make mistakes and not to be perfect at everything. They have to become more flexible, accept themselves, and find more balance in their lives.

Relationships

When it comes to relationships, they have high expectations of themselves and their partners. They appreciate partners who are honest and reliable. They must be careful not to be too critical and demanding, as this type of behavior could strain their relationships.

2. *The Helper/Giver*

Helpers are kind people, who enjoy helping others. However, if they are in an unhealthy state, they can be codependent, manipulative, or people pleasers.

Characteristics

The Helper is good at making others feel loved, and they're good at making friends. They're good team players as they're always prepared to take on extra work and help others who are struggling.

Fears

Helpers fear being unwanted or unloved. They may worry that if they don't offer assistance or support, they will lose the affection of others.

Desires

The Helper wants to feel loved, appreciated, and valued. They long for deep emotional connections and meaningful relationships.

Communication Style

Helpers are warm, nurturing, and good listeners. They are empathetic and good at comforting others. Their communication style could sometimes be regarded as manipulative if they use providing help to someone as a way to get recognition.

Strengths

Helpers genuinely care about others. They can anticipate the needs of others and provide help in practical ways. Their nurturing nature can create a supportive environment.

Potential Challenges

They can struggle with setting boundaries and neglect their own needs. They tend to become overly dependent on the approval and appreciation of others. They could also suppress their negative emotions to promote harmony in their relationships.

Growth and Development

Helpers have to learn to prioritize self-care and establish healthy boundaries. They must learn that they're not only worthy when they help others. They also need to attend to their own needs and desires, which will enable them to express their generosity in a more authentic way.

Relationships

Helpers make good partners and friends who want to contribute to the well-being of their loved ones. They must take care not to become codependent and need to accept that mutual give-and-take is important in relationships.

3. Achiever/Performer

The Achiever/Performer is a dynamic and driven personality. These types are confident and charismatic and thrive on the validation they receive from others.

Characteristics

The energetic and confident Achiever is driven by a desire to succeed and wants to receive recognition for what they accomplish. They are highly motivated and will strive for excellence at work.

Fears

Achievers fear failure, and they don't want to be seen as incompetent. They also fear being overlooked or being seen as irrelevant by others, for example, at work.

Desires

The Achiever wants recognition, validation, and admiration. They want their achievements and success to be acknowledged.

Communication Style

Achievers can be articulate and persuasive. Their enthusiasm and passion make them charismatic communicators. They make good managers, as they can inspire others and they tend to focus on tangible results.

Strengths

They are good employees, as they have an excellent work ethic, and they're reliable, productive workers. They're also determined and good problem solvers.

Potential Challenges

Their work ethic can also cause challenges for Achievers. It could cause them to become workaholics and neglect their personal well-being and relationships with their friends and family. Constantly chasing their goals could lead to burnout.

The Achiever can also become over-focused on validation from others, and as a result, may neglect their inner needs.

Growth and Development

Achievers can experience personal growth by developing their self-awareness and being aware of the motivations that are driving their behavior.

They need to develop a more balanced approach to success.

Relationships

Achievers look for partners and friends who support and admire them. They need to work on developing empathy and vulnerability, as this will help them when it comes to developing better relationships.

4. *Individualist/Romantic*

The Individualist is a creative individual with a rich inner world.

Characteristics

These creative people want to express their unique identity. They want to be appreciated for their individuality.

Fears

The Individualist fears not having a unique personal identity. They want to be seen as special and to connect to others in a meaningful way.

Desires

The desires of the Individualist are based around self-expression and being authentic. They thrive in environments and relationships that allow them to express their individuality and creativity. The

Individualist wants to be understood and appreciated for their unique perspective.

Communication Style

They like to express themselves in a poetic and expressive way and like to use metaphors and images to portray their emotions. They are intuitive and can pick up on emotional cues. They're usually empathetic, and emotionally intelligent.

Strengths

The strength of the Individualist is to tap into their rich inner world and express their emotions through creativity. Their unique perspective helps them to see beauty in unexpected places.

Potential Challenges

The Individualist can be self-absorbed and doubt themselves. They tend to compare themselves to others and then end up feeling inadequate. Their personal growth can be obstructed by their desire to be perfect and the fear that they're not unique. They need to work at developing resilience and self-compassion.

Growth and Development

Individualists need to become more resilient and realize that they don't have to rely on external validation. They need to self-reflect and become more self-aware. It's important for them to find healthy outlets for their creativity and emotions.

Relationships

Individualists want authentic relationships, and they value emotional depth. They could withdraw and become moody when they feel people don't understand them.

5. *Investigator/Observer*

The Investigator has a thirst for knowledge.

Characteristics

Investigators are curious, observant, and analytical. They value their privacy and independence.

Fears

The investigator fears being seen as incompetent and overwhelmed by the demands of the outside world. They collect knowledge and work at improving their expertise in an effort not to be seen as incompetent. They also fear opening up to others and making themselves vulnerable.

Desires

Investigators want to develop a deep understanding of themselves and the world around them. They enjoy intellectual stimulation and want the freedom to pursue their passions and interests. They want privacy and to explore their own ideas without interference.

Communication Style

The Investigator communicates in a clear manner and always focuses on facts and information. They can experience difficult concepts and theories in a logical and user-friendly way. They enjoy in-depth discussions where they can exchange intellectual ideas. Investigators could struggle with sharing their emotions.

Strengths

Investigators are good analytical thinkers, and they have excellent attention to detail. Their strengths are gathering information and doing thorough investigations. Their self-sufficiency helps them to deal with challenges in a resilient way.

Potential Challenges

Investigators have a tendency to become emotionally attached and overthink. They could focus too much on gathering knowledge and, as a result, become disconnected from others. They need to learn to balance their search for knowledge with forming meaningful connections with others.

Growth and Development

Growth for the Investigator would involve cultivating emotional intelligence, stepping out of their comfort zones, and forming more connections with others. Developing empathy and vulnerability allows them to connect on a deeper level with those around them. They should embrace uncertainty and take calculated risks to help them overcome their fear of incompetence.

Relationships

Investigators appreciate partners who respect their need for solitude and share their intellectual interests. They could struggle with emotional intimacy, and they could need to work on expressing their emotions.

6. The Loyalist/Skeptic

The Loyalist is responsible, loyal, and vigilant.

Characteristics

The Loyalist is good at identifying risks and dangers in their environment, which means they're excellent at preparing for worst-case scenarios. They are hardworking and diligent people who appreciate receiving support and guidance from trusted authority figures.

Fears

The Loyalist fears feeling insecure and unsupported. They could feel overwhelmed in situations where there is a lot of uncertainty, as they prefer stable environments. They often second-guess their decisions and can look at others to reassure them.

Desires

The Loyalist wants stability and certainty. They want systems and relationships they can depend on. They want to feel like they belong in a group and that they're accepted and validated.

Communication Style

Loyalists tend to think before they speak, as they are aware of the effects their words may have on others.

Loyalists are good listeners and can offer other practical solutions to problems.

Strengths

Loyalists are dependable and dedicated. They make good employees, and they're committed to their tasks and relationships.

They're excellent at anticipating problems and finding practical solutions to them. Loyalists also make good team players, as they value working with others and they support their group's goals.

Potential Challenges

Loyalists may struggle with anxiety and fear. Their vigilance can lead to overthinking and a habit of worrying. They could also be indecisive and second-guess themselves when they make decisions. As the Loyalist is so cautious, it can hamper their ability to embrace change and take risks.

Growth and Development

When it comes to personal growth, the Loyalist needs to become more confident in their abilities. They should challenge themselves by stepping out of their comfort zones. They need to become self-reliant and trust their own judgment. They have to come to accept that uncertainty is just a part of life.

Relationships

Trust and security are important to Loyalists in relationships. They will benefit from open communication in relationships.

7. The Enthusiast/Epicure

The energetic and lively Enthusiast is usually an optimistic and positive individual.

Characteristics

The Enthusiast is usually adventurous and constantly looks for exciting new experiences. Enthusiasts are usually forward-thinking, and they're filled with ideas and possibilities for the future.

Fears

The Enthusiast fears missing out on exciting experiences. They don't like feeling restricted and prefer to keep their options open.

The Enthusiast also fears emotional pain and discomfort. They choose to focus on positive emotions, and they avoid confronting their deeper feelings and difficult experiences they may have had.

They also fear boredom or becoming stuck in monotonous routines.

Desires

The Enthusiast frequently experiences a desire for freedom and fulfillment. They want to feel that there are various possibilities available to them in their lives.

The Enthusiast has a strong desire to feel joy and happiness. They will look for activities and relationships that will make them feel that way.

Enthusiasts also desire a positive and comfortable environment. They will look for pleasure and aim to avoid emotional and physical pain.

Communication Style

Enthusiasts have a lively and engaging communication style. They tend to use expressive gestures and vivid language.

They enjoy sharing their experiences and ideas with others, and their stories can be full of excitement.

Enthusiasts will find humor in different situations and can even use it to entertain those around them.

They also have a tendency to dominate conversations and could interrupt other speakers. They usually have many interests and ideas, and they can jump around from topic to topic when they're having a conversation.

Strengths

Enthusiasts have a gift for seeing opportunities and possibilities. They are optimistic, and their energy can inspire others and uplift them.

Enthusiasts are optimistic and inspire others. Their energy is contagious, and they can make social settings more exciting.

Enthusiasts are also versatile and quick to adapt to new situations.

Potential Challenges

Enthusiasts may find it difficult to face and deal with negative emotions. They usually choose to suppress their negative emotions and choose instead to focus on the positive ones.

They can be impulsive and may find it difficult to deal with long-term projects.

They may use distractions to keep themselves from having to face challenging situations or confront their deeper emotions.

They could struggle to prioritize and focus on one idea at a time.

They can overlook details and neglect their responsibilities. Enthusiasts don't enjoy being involved with repetitive tasks.

Growth and Development

Enthusiasts need to learn to stay present and deal with their difficult emotions. Learning to deal with uncomfortable emotions can help them with developing self-awareness and experiencing emotional growth.

Enthusiasts need to develop the ability to commit and work on their long-term goals. They need to learn to complete projects, even if the excitement they initially had fades.

Enthusiasts need to learn to tolerate discomfort and develop resilience.

Enthusiasts can work on experiencing sustainable happiness by finding contentment in the present moment and appreciating the simple things in life.

Enthusiasts need to get in touch with their deeper emotions and delve into meaningful experiences instead of constantly looking for continuous external validation.

Relationships

Enthusiasts are fun and playful partners. They're spontaneous and love exploring new experiences with their partners.

However, they could struggle with commitment and might want to escape from emotional intensity. They could need support to help them stay present in the relationship. They need to work at being emotionally present for their partners.

8. *The Challenger/Protector*

Challengers are strong, assertive characters, with a desire to control others.

Characteristics

The Challenger tends to have a determined and self-confident approach to life. They are protective and loyal, and they do their best to protect the people in their lives.

They're independent and tend to rely on themselves. They have a lot of energy and tend to take charge in difficult situations.

They are courageous and can be resilient when it comes to facing challenges.

Fears

Challengers fear being controlled or manipulated. They don't want to be controlled by others, and it's important to them to remain independent.

They fear they will be viewed as weak and vulnerable by others. They also struggle to trust others, as they fear they will be taken advantage of.

Desires

Challengers want to control their own lives and make their own decisions.

They have a desire for justice and want to see fairness in the world around them. They want safety and security and will take care of the people in their lives.

Communication Style

Challengers will communicate their thoughts and opinions clearly and openly. They are assertive and confident and may come across as demanding.

Challengers value authenticity and honesty. They're also not scared of confrontation and are willing to engage in it if they regard something as an injustice.

Strengths

Challengers are natural leaders and can inspire and motivate others. They are good at taking decisive action to overcome challenges.

Challengers are also results-oriented and driven. They are highly motivated to achieve their goals and are good at confronting challenging situations.

Potential Challenges

Challengers could be domineering and controlling. They can struggle to let go of control and give others an opportunity to lead.

They don't like asking for help, and it can be difficult for them to show vulnerability. They choose to rely on themselves, even when they're suffering.

They can be impatient with what they perceive as being weakness or incompetence in others and show a lack of understanding of the challenges faced by others.

Challengers also don't like embracing emotional sensitivity, and they struggle with acknowledging and expressing their emotions. They're more likely to focus on practical actions and solutions.

Growth and Development

Challengers need to trust others in a bid to form deeper connections in their relationships. They need to learn to balance their assertiveness with empathy and consider the needs and perspectives of others.

They need to recognize that there is value in collaborating and sharing power. Challengers can grow, learn to delegate, and share responsibilities.

They need to work on growing their emotional awareness and emotional intelligence. Challengers also need to explore the deeper reasons why they have a desire for control. They need to find healthier ways to express their autonomy and assertiveness.

Relationships

Challengers are protective and reliable partners. They could struggle to let go of control in a relationship and could need to work on shared decision-making.

The partners of Challengers can support them by providing them with a safe space to express their emotions and vulnerability.

9. The Peacemaker/Mediator

Peacemakers are laid-back, easy, and accommodating people.

Characteristics

They usually desire a calm and peaceful atmosphere. Peacemakers tend to avoid conflict and confrontation. They could struggle to assert themselves.

They prefer peaceful environments that are free from disruption. They could adopt the viewpoints of others to maintain harmony, which means they may lose touch with their own desires.

Fears

The Peacemaker fears conflict and being overlooked and disregarded in relationships. They fear losing connection with others and becoming disconnected from themselves. This could cause them to avoid confrontation, and they might not assert their needs and opinions, as they would rather maintain harmonious relationships.

Desires

The Peacemaker wants to create a peaceful and harmonious environment. They want to feel at one with others.

Communication Style

Peacemakers are gentle and diplomatic communicators. They are attentive listeners but could struggle with expressing their viewpoints, as they will go along with others to keep the peace. They could use indirect language to avoid conflict.

Strengths

Peacemakers are natural mediators. They have the ability to see multiple perspectives and find common ground. They are good at connecting people and resolving conflicts.

Others usually find peacemakers calming and approachable.

Peacemakers have the ability to understand and empathize with people. They have genuine empathy for others.

Potential Challenges

Their tendency to avoid conflict can lead to unexpressed frustration when conflicts aren't addressed directly. Avoidance can also lead to passive-aggressive behavior.

They could neglect their own needs and sacrifice their well-being. This leads to dissatisfaction. Peacemakers can also resist change to maintain their stability and harmony.

Growth and Development

For Peacemakers to grow, they need to recognize and value their own needs and desires. They should be able to assert themselves without being afraid or feeling guilty.

Peacemakers should also focus on increasing their self-awareness, which will help them identify and address the emotions they could be avoiding.

They should also practice setting boundaries and express their opinions and desires in an authentic way, even if it may cause discomfort for others.

Relationships

Peacemakers are typically supportive, accepting, and accommodating. They should just aim to resolve conflicts and assert their own needs in relationships.

Practical Exercise: Improve Communication with the Different Enneagram Types

Improving your communication with the different Enneagram types can help you enhance understanding, reduce conflict, and also form stronger relationships with different types of people.

The aim of this exercise is to develop better communication skills and deepen understanding when you have to deal with people from different Enneagram types. It can be particularly useful in a work environment.

Instructions

Follow these steps for this group exercise:

- You will first need to find participants who know something about the Enneagram and are interested in learning more.

- Each Enneagram type needs to be explained and discussed. You may have people in the group who don't know that much about the subject.

- Choose one of the Enneagram types and choose a facilitator to guide the exercise. This person must then give an overview of the Enneagram type that has been chosen.

- The participants must then share their experiences in interacting with people of that type.

- Participants need to be able to ask each other questions.

- The group needs to discuss communication strategies that could be effective in interacting with a certain Enneagram type.

- The participants should do role-playing exercises where they simulate conversations that involve the different Enneagram types. They need to practice the communication strategies that were discussed.

- If you have the time, you should try to do the exercise with as many Enneagram types as possible.

- In the end, the participants should have a group discussion regarding what they've learned from the experience.

Key Takeaways

- The Enneagram can help us communicate better by helping us understand how our own personality type and other types communicate. It can enable us to express ourselves more clearly.

- Knowledge of the Enneagram can help us reduce misunderstandings in our relationships and build empathetic relationships that are based on respect.

- You first need to familiarize yourself with how the Enneagram system works if you're going to use it to determine your personality type.

- Self-reflection can help you determine your Enneagram type. Introspection can help you analyze your thoughts and emotions, as well as your behavior.

- Childhood patterns can provide valuable insight into Enneagram types. Early experiences have a lot to do with shaping the development of your personality. We should reflect on how our childhood has influenced our behavior and outlook.

- Enneagram assessments can help you determine your type. There are many tests online, but you should only regard them as a supplemental resource for determining your Enneagram type.

- The Enneagram can also help you deal with complicated relationships. If you understand your type, you'll become more aware of your patterns and tendencies in different relationships.

- Each Enneagram type has its own needs and preferences.

Chapter 4:

Improving Personal and Professional Relationships

The Enneagram can be a powerful tool in the workplace for fostering better communication, teamwork, and productivity.

To achieve a healthy environment for their team members in the workplace, managers must be able to understand the personalities and working styles of their team members.

If there is no real understanding of how employees function, and the professional environment is toxic, the business is much more likely to experience a high staff turnover.

The Benefit of the Enneagram for Professional Teams

The Enneagram can be very beneficial for professional teams. It can encourage people to improve their communication skills in various ways.

The Enneagram encourages people to become more self-aware and develop a better understanding of their strengths and weaknesses. People are encouraged to become aware of areas where they need to grow and to take responsibility for their communication patterns and actions. Greater self-awareness will also lead to improved interactions with their coworkers.

The Enneagram can help employees understand their team members better. It makes it easier to gain insight into the motivations, communication styles, and fears of the team members and can help them value each other's diverse perspectives. This will improve teamwork and productivity.

It can help employees connect better with each other. Communication strategies can be adapted to suit the needs of the different team members. If people can connect better with their coworkers, it can reduce misunderstandings and conflict and enhance productivity.

Workplace conflict is often the result of poor communication. Employees not only need better communication skills, but they must also be aware of their biases and the cultural differences within teams. Knowing the Enneagram can also help teams to resolve conflicts faster.

Team members who don't communicate well may also struggle to work together. There might not be direct conflict, but if there's a lack of understanding, it could lead to missed deadlines and unsuccessful projects. Effective collaboration is especially important during a time when more people are working remotely.

The Enneagram can help to identify the unique strengths and talents of the team members. This knowledge can be used to structure team assignments to make the most of each team member's strengths, which will create a more balanced and productive team. If tasks are assigned according to the strengths of the different team members, the team will perform better, and everyone will have greater job satisfaction.

It can also be a tool for personal and professional development and growth. Organizations can offer Enneagram workshops, training, or coaching to support employees' growth and self-awareness. By understanding their Enneagram type, individuals can identify areas for improvement, develop new skills, and enhance their overall performance in the workplace.

The Enneagram encourages empathy and understanding among team members. By appreciating the fears, motivations, and communication styles of colleagues, individuals can develop empathy and compassion for each other. This cultivates a positive and supportive work environment and will strengthen trust between the team members.

It can also provide valuable insights into leadership styles and preferences. By understanding their own Enneagram type and the types of their team members, leaders can adapt their leadership approach to better support and motivate individuals. They can tailor communication, delegate tasks effectively, and create an environment that fosters growth and engagement.

How the Different Enneagram Types Approach Their Work and Relationships

Each Enneagram type approaches its work and relationships with distinct motivations, strengths, and challenges.

Type 1—The Perfectionist/Reformer

Perfectionists, or Reformers, are diligent and strive for excellence at work. They have high standards and will take on leadership roles. They are usually fair and can provide constructive feedback to help others grow.

Perfectionists usually approach their work with a strong sense of responsibility, high standards, and a desire for excellence. It is very important to them to do things right.

The Perfectionist has a keen eye for detail and a natural inclination to identify and correct errors or inconsistencies. They aim to deliver accurate and precise work.

Perfectionists are highly committed and have a strong work ethic. They take their responsibilities seriously and are dependable team members.

They set high standards for themselves and others. They aim to continuously improve in their work. Perfectionists are motivated by a desire to make a positive impact and create meaningful contributions.

Perfectionists are principled individuals who seek fairness, justice, and integrity in their work. They often become advocates for social or organizational change.

Perfectionists approach their work relationships with the same desire for excellence. They are professional and dependable team members.

Perfectionists will advocate for equitable treatment and ethical practices within their work relationships. They may speak up against injustices or unfair practices to promote a more harmonious and just work environment.

Perfectionists could offer constructive feedback to their colleagues with the intention of helping them grow and improve. They value personal and professional development and want to see positive change. However, they should be careful to deliver feedback in a tactful way.

Under Severe Stress

When under stress, Type 1 tends to move to Type 4. They can become their own worst critics as they feel hopeless.

Type 2—The Helper/Giver

The Helper, or Giver, approaches their job with a focus on supporting and assisting others.

They are high achievers in roles that allow them to help, guide, or mentor others. They are satisfied by making a positive impact and meeting the needs of those they work with.

Helpers are team players and value collaboration. They thrive in environments where they can work closely with others and contribute to the success of the team. They are often adept at fostering co-operation and building strong relationships within the workplace.

Helpers are empathetic and highly attuned to the needs and emotions of those around them. They can anticipate and respond to the needs of their colleagues, creating a supportive and harmonious work environment.

Helpers possess excellent interpersonal skills, allowing them to connect with others on a deep level. They are experts at building rapport, listening actively, and creating a safe space for open communication.

They may struggle with setting boundaries, which could cause them to be abused in the workplace, as they also tend to overextend themselves and neglect their own needs. It's important for them to practice self-care and establish healthy boundaries to prevent burnout.

Under Severe Stress

When under stress, Type 2 can display Type 8 behavior. Stress can cause a Type 2 to become aggressive and try to control or blame others.

Type 3—The Achiever/Performer

The Achiever, or Performer, is focused on success, achievement, and recognition.

Achievers are highly motivated by goals and strive to excel in their work. They are driven, ambitious, and determined to achieve success. They often seek out challenging projects and are willing to put in the necessary effort to accomplish their objectives.

Achievers are focused on outcomes and tend to prioritize efficiency and productivity. They excel at organizing their time and resources effectively to maximize their output. They have a natural ability to identify and seize opportunities for advancement.

Achievers can adapt to different work environments and often have versatile skill sets. They quickly learn new skills and competencies, which helps them thrive in a variety of roles and industries.

They are conscious of their personal and professional image and want to present themselves in a competent manner. They also care about their appearance.

Achievers will strive to accomplish shared objectives or personal growth together with their coworkers. They're good at networking and relationship building, which can help them advance in the work environment and achieve their professional goals.

Achievers are also competitive by nature and can try to outperform others. They will try to establish themselves as the best or most accomplished in their field.

Under Severe Stress

When under stress, Type 3 will move to Type 9. They can lose focus and become preoccupied.

Type 4—The Individualist/Romantic

The Individualist, or Romantic, approaches their job with a focus on self-expression, authenticity, and depth.

Individualists are creative and often seek work that allows them to express their unique perspectives and talents. They thrive in roles that encourage personal growth, innovation, and artistic expression.

They are also motivated by a desire for depth and meaning in their work. Individualists want to engage with projects or tasks that align with their values and allow them to make a significant impact or explore complex ideas.

Individualists have a heightened emotional awareness, which often translates into their work. They bring a depth of emotion and sensitivity to their creative endeavors, contributing a unique and personal touch to their work output.

They want to be seen as authentic and distinct. Individualists don't want to conform to societal norms, and they could be drawn to unconventional or nontraditional work environments.

Under Severe Stress

When experiencing stress, Type 4 can move to Type 2. They can become overly dependent on others and look for validation.

Type 5—The Investigator/Observer

The Investigator, or Observer, focuses on knowledge, understanding, and autonomy when it comes to their work.

Since Investigators have a deep desire for knowledge and understanding, they do well in roles that allow them to explore complicated subjects, conduct research, or analyze information. They are often drawn to work that requires expertise or specialized knowledge.

Investigators highly value their autonomy and prefer working independently. They are self-reliant and prefer to have control over their time, space, and work processes. They thrive in environments that provide them with the freedom to pursue their intellectual interests.

They have a natural inclination to observe and analyze their surroundings. Investigators are keen observers and excel at gathering information and getting valuable insights from it. They have a methodical and systematic approach to their work.

Investigators often require private and personal space to concentrate and recharge. They may prefer to work in quiet, secluded environments where they can focus on their tasks without interruptions.

The Investigator will appreciate work relationships that provide them with intellectual stimulation and the opportunity to share knowledge and ideas. They enjoy exploring complex subjects with the input of others.

Under Severe Stress

Work stress can cause Type 5 to become more like Type 7. They can become distracted and become detached from the team.

Type 6—The Loyalist/Skeptic

The Loyalist, or Skeptic, approaches their work and relationships with a focus on security, loyalty, and preparedness.

Loyalists have a strong sense of responsibility and take their work commitments seriously. They are reliable, dependable, and dedicated to fulfilling their obligations. They do well in roles that involve planning, risk management, and ensuring the security and stability of the work environment.

They are often meticulous and pay close attention to details. Loyalists take a cautious and thoughtful approach to their work, ensuring that tasks are completed accurately and comprehensively. They excel in roles that require attention to regulations, protocols, and adherence to guidelines.

Loyalists prioritize security and stability in their work environment. They appreciate structures and clear expectations. Loyalists may be diligent in following procedures and seeking out information or guidance to mitigate potential risks.

Loyalists value collaboration and working as part of a team. They thrive in environments that foster a sense of belonging and camaraderie. They are loyal and committed team members who contribute to the group's success.

Under Severe Stress

Under stress, Type 6 can become like Type 3. They tend to disregard their feelings and they may display workaholic tendencies.

Type 7—The Enthusiast/Epicure

The Enthusiast, or Epicure, approaches work and relationships with a focus on joy, variety, and optimism.

The Enthusiast thrives in work environments that offer excitement, variety, and opportunities for new experiences. They enjoy exploring different projects, ideas, and challenges. They are often enthusiastic about their work and bring a sense of energy and positivity to their tasks.

Enthusiasts are often highly creative and innovative. They excel in roles that allow them to think outside the box and come up with new ideas or solutions. They enjoy brainstorming and they do well in environments that encourage creative thinking.

They are adept at multitasking and adaptability. They have a natural ability to juggle multiple projects or responsibilities simultaneously. They are quick to adapt to changes and enjoy learning new skills or taking on new roles.

Enthusiasts approach their work with optimism and a positive attitude. They focus on possibilities and opportunities rather than dwelling on challenges or setbacks. They often inspire and motivate others with their enthusiasm and upbeat energy.

Under Severe Stress

When experiencing work stress, Type 7 can become more like Type 1. They tend to be critical and narrow-minded.

Type 8—The Challenger/Protector

The Challenger, or Protector, approaches work and relationships with a focus on power, control, and assertiveness.

Challengers are known for their assertiveness and decisiveness in the workplace. They are confident in their abilities and often take charge of situations. They thrive in roles that allow them to lead, make decisions, and take control.

They are usually highly focused on achieving results. Challengers are action-oriented and excel at driving projects forward. They have a natural ability to set clear goals, establish strategies, and motivate others to achieve success.

Challengers value direct and straightforward communication. They are known for their candid and no-nonsense approach to interactions. They appreciate when others communicate openly and honestly with them, and they will do the same in return.

Protectors value their autonomy and independence in the workplace. They prefer having the freedom to make decisions and take ownership of their work. They may resist authority or control from others and prefer to be self-directed.

Under Severe Stress

When experiencing work stress, Type 8 can become more like Type 5. They can withdraw and lose touch with their emotions.

Type 9—The Peacemaker/Mediator

The Peacemaker, or Mediator, approaches work and relationships with a focus on harmony, cooperation, and maintaining inner peace.

Mediators have a natural inclination toward co-operation and harmony in the workplace. They value a peaceful and pleasant work environment and will work hard at maintaining positive relationships with their colleagues.

Peacemakers have a natural ability to mediate and resolve conflicts. They are skilled at finding common ground and facilitating compromise among team members. They excel in roles that require diplomacy.

They are also adaptable and flexible in their work approach. They can easily adjust to changing circumstances or requirements. They value a work environment that allows them to have a sense of autonomy and freedom to contribute in their own way.

Peacemakers may hesitate to assert themselves or express their own needs or opinions if it risks creating tension. It's important for them to find a balance between maintaining harmony and advocating for their own interests.

Under Severe Stress

When experiencing intense work stress, Type 9 will move to Type 6. They can become anxious and indecisive. They can also start to doubt themselves.

Ideal Job Roles for the Different Enneagram Types

People with different Enneagram types all have qualities and strengths that make them more suitable for specific job roles.

Type 1—The Perfectionist/Reformer

The Perfectionist's personality attributes make them suitable for the following roles:

- **project management:** Since Perfectionists are organized, responsible and efficient, they excel at project management roles. They also have high attention to detail, they maintain high standards, and they're good at meeting deadlines.

- **quality control/assurance:** Their high attention to detail makes them excellent for quality assurance roles. These are jobs that could allow them to use their meticulousness, such as in manufacturing, software testing, or auditing.

- **legal professions:** Perfectionists have a strong desire for justice and high moral standards, which makes them suited for careers in compliance, advocacy, and law.

- **research and analysis:** Perfectionists also excel in roles that require critical thinking and fact-checking. Careers in research, data analysis, or investigative roles can allow them to apply their analytical skills and pursue knowledge.

- **non-profit or humanitarian work:** Perfectionists also want to make a positive impact. They could find it fulfilling to work for non-profit organizations or do humanitarian work.

Type 2—The Helper/Giver

The Helper's personality attributes make them suitable for the following roles:

- **counseling or therapy:** Helpers are empathetic and understand other people's needs and emotions. They naturally want to help and support others. Roles in counseling or therapy allow them to use their listening skills and natural compassion to help others with healing.

- **healthcare professions:** Jobs in nursing, caregiving, social work, or any other healthcare-related profession will also allow them to use their natural compassion and empathy.

- **human resources:** Helpers are also skilled at building relationships. Jobs in human resources, such as recruitment, training, or employee engagement allow them to use their skills in connecting with others and creating positive work environments.

- **customer service:** Their natural inclination to provide excellent service, empathize with customers, and solve their challenges make them suitable for customer service roles.

- **teaching or mentoring:** Helpers are also good mentors, and they enjoy watching others grow. Teaching, tutoring, and mentoring allow them to use their nurturing nature and passion for supporting the development of others.

Type 3—The Achiever/Performer

Achievers' personality attributes make them suitable for the following roles:

- **sales and marketing:** Achievers are charismatic, persuasive, and highly motivated. They're great at promoting products or services, building relationships with clients, and achieving sales targets. They can be very successful in sales and marketing roles.

- **leadership and management:** Achievers are ambitious and self-assured. They have the natural strengths to make good leaders and can inspire and motivate others.

- **entrepreneurship:** Achievers are suited for entrepreneurship, as they are ambitious, adaptable, and they enjoy risk-taking. They are self-motivated and have a desire to succeed on their own terms.

- **public relations and media:** Achievers are also good communicators who are excellent at public speaking. Roles in public relations, media, or communications allow them to use their networking skills and charisma.

- **event planning and project management:** Achievers also have the ability to manage multiple responsibilities, which makes them suited to event planning and project management.

Type 4—The Individualist/Romantic

The Individualist's personality attributes make them suitable for the following roles:

- **creative professions:** Individualists are artistic and creative. They are innovative and have emotional depth, which helps them to excel as artists, writers, designers, or poets.

- **counselors and therapists:** Individualists are attuned to their own and others' emotions. They can connect with others on an emotional level, which makes them well-suited for roles in counseling and therapy.

- **creative directors:** Individualists have a unique vision, and their innovative ideas make them ideal for creative directing roles.

- **social work or advocacy:** Individualists have a passion for justice, which also makes them ideal for social work or community organizing.

- **entrepreneurship or freelancing:** Individualists are independent and are often driven by a desire to create something unique and authentic. They are good entrepreneurs, as they can bring their creative ideas to life while staying autonomous at the same time.

Type 5—The Investigator/Observer

The Investigator's personality attributes make them suitable for the following roles:

- **research and analysis:** Roles that involve scientific research and data analysis can allow Investigators to use their analytical skills.

- **information technology:** Investigators have a natural aptitude for technology and complex systems. They are good at problem-solving and find innovative solutions. Roles in software development, cybersecurity, IT support, or systems analysis are a good fit for their logical thinking.

- **writing and editing:** Investigators also thrive in environments that allow them to express themselves through writing, editing, and proofreading. Roles in technical writing, copywriting, editing, or content creation can allow them to use their research abilities and their ability to communicate complex ideas clearly.

- **academia and teaching:** Investigators also love learning and can find fulfillment in teaching others about their specialized knowledge. Roles in academia, teaching, or training can allow them to share their knowledge with others.

- **freelancing or consulting:** Investigators enjoy working independently and they can thrive in roles as freelancers or consultants where they can pursue their interests in a flexible way.

Type 6—The Loyalist/Skeptic

The Loyalist's personality attributes make them suitable for the following roles:

- **risk assessment and management:** The Loyalist is good at identifying potential risks and planning for them. They are diligent, cautious, and thorough. They do well at jobs in risk assessment, compliance, or project management as these allow them to use their skills to identify and mitigate potential risks.

- **emergency response and crisis management:** The Loyalist excels in high-pressure situations, as they're capable of staying calm and thinking quickly. They'll do well in roles in emergency response, crisis management, or disaster relief.

- **human resources and organizational development:** Individualists are also good at assessing and understanding people's needs. They value creating supportive work environments and can use their skills in human resources jobs, organizational development, or employee engagement. They can contribute to creating positive workplace cultures.

- **administration and operations:** Individualists are also organized and responsible. They excel in administrative tasks, operations management, and coordinating operations to ensure that things run smoothly.

- **law enforcement and security:** Individualists have a strong sense of justice and want to protect others. They thrive in roles that involve maintaining law and order, as well as the safety and security of others.

Type 7—The Enthusiast/Epicure

The Enthusiast's personality attributes make them suitable for the following roles:

- **sales and marketing:** Enthusiasts are charismatic, energetic, and persuasive. They're good at working with people, networking, and promoting products or services. Enthusiasts can make contributions in roles that involve sales, marketing, or business development.

- **event planning and hospitality:** Enthusiasts have a talent for creating and organizing experiences. They enjoy connecting with people and making sure that they enjoy themselves. They can use their talents in roles that involve event planning, hospitality management, or tourism. These types of jobs will provide them with the opportunity to use their creative talents.

- **entrepreneurship and start-ups:** Enthusiasts are also risk-takers and innovators. They enjoy challenges and starting their own business can provide them with freedom and excitement.

- **coaching and personal development:** Enthusiasts desire personal growth and exploration. They excel in roles that involve helping others achieve personal growth and reaching their goals.

- **creative industries:** Enthusiasts have strong imaginations, and they love exploring and new experiences. They excel in creative roles that involve writing, design, photography, or performing arts. These roles give them the freedom to express themselves and explore different perspectives.

Type 8—The Challenger/Protector

The Challenger's personality attributes make them suitable for the following roles:

- **leadership and executive roles:** Challengers are naturally confident and assertive leaders. They can make tough decisions and lead teams. They do well in jobs like CEOs, directors, or managers.

- **entrepreneurship and business ownership:** Challengers are independent and willing to take risks. They do well at running their own businesses as they can use their strategic vision.

- **advocacy and activism:** Challengers also have a strong sense of justice and want to protect the rights of others. They do well in roles that involve standing up against injustice. Positions in social justice organizations, activism, or advocacy groups will allow them to live out their desire to create positive change.

- **sales and negotiation:** Challengers can be persuasive and assertive communicators. They can present their ideas with confidence and influence others with ease. They usually do well in roles that involve sales and negotiations.

- **crisis and conflict management:** Challengers are comfortable in high-pressure situations, and they can manage conflict. They can take charge and maintain control in tough situations. They can use their assertiveness and decisive nature in roles that involve crisis management, conflict resolution, or mediation.

Type 9—The Peacemaker/Mediator

The Peacemaker's personality attributes make them suitable for the following roles:

- **mediation and conflict resolution:** Peacemakers do well in roles that involve resolving conflicts, facilitating dialogue, and finding common ground. They have strong listening skills, and they're skilled at creating peaceful environments. Roles in mediation, community organizing, or diplomatic services will allow them to use their skills.

- **counseling and therapy:** Peacemakers understand and accept others. They can provide support and guidance to others, and they can make a contribution by helping people deal with their personal challenges. They can use their compassionate nature for positions in counseling, therapy, or social work.

- **human resources and organizational development:** Peacemakers have strong interpersonal skills and they're skilled at getting people to work together. They excel in jobs that involve conflict management and ensuring a harmonious work environment. Positions in human resources, organizational development, or employee relations will allow them to use these skills.

- **non-profit and social justice work:** Peacemakers also have a strong sense of justice and a desire to promote social change. They're good at working toward a greater cause and providing support to marginalized communities. Jobs in non-profit organizations, advocacy groups, or community service will allow them to use their empathy.

- **administrative and coordinating roles:** Challengers have excellent organizational skills and they do well in roles that involve coordinating tasks, managing schedules, and ensuring smooth operations. They have the ability to bring people together efficiently. Project management, administrative support, or event coordination will allow them to use their organizational and administrative skills.

How Using the Enneagram Can Increase Job Satisfaction

The Enneagram can be a valuable tool for improving job satisfaction and fulfillment by providing insights into personal motivations, strengths, and areas for growth.

You can use the Enneagram to increase your job satisfaction in the following ways:

- It can help you understand your own patterns of behavior, motivations, and underlying fears or desires. By gaining this self-awareness, you can align your choice of profession with your core values and find roles that you find personally fulfilling. It can help you find a career that is satisfying to you.

- The Enneagram can also help you identify your strengths and growth areas. Understanding your Enneagram type can help you use your strengths in your job roles, which can help you feel competent and accomplished. It will also show you areas in which you need to grow.

- You'll be able to understand your coworkers' communication styles better, so you should be able to improve your collaboration and resolve conflicts more easily.

- The Enneagram can help people find work that aligns with their passions and values. If you understand your motivations and desires, you can look for roles that provide you with meaning and fulfillment.

- Knowing your Enneagram can also help you understand how you deal with stress and cope with challenges. If you understand what triggers your stress reactions, you can develop strategies to deal with stress better and create a healthier work-life balance. This can help you maintain job satisfaction and prevent burnout.

- If you know your Enneagram type, it's also easier to work on career planning and development. You can get more insight into career paths and work environments, roles, and tasks that will be the most fulfilling for your Enneagram type.

How the Enneagram Helped People from Different Backgrounds to Work Together

A diverse creative team was working for a publishing agency called BriteBooks. The team members all had different personalities, communication styles, and ways of doing tasks. While they all had unique strengths, at times they found themselves struggling to work together effectively.

One day, their manager, Tom, introduced them to the Enneagram in a bid to improve their communication and ability to work together as a team. The team realized that they had to foster better working relationships with each other, and they embraced the Enneagram to help them do this.

They started by taking the Enneagram test and discovered that each team member fell into a different personality type. Mark was a Type 1, known as the Perfectionist, who always wanted to improve processes and achieve excellence. Sophia was a Type 2, the Helper, with a nurturing and supportive nature. Emma, who was driven and successful, embodied the qualities of Type 3, the Achiever. Richard, a Type 5, the Investigator, was an analytical thinker who craved knowledge and depth. Sarah, a Type 9, the Peacemaker, valued harmony and collaboration.

With this new understanding, it was easier for the team members to appreciate each other's motivations and strengths. They began to realize that their different perspectives and approaches could improve the team's overall performance.

Mark used his attention to detail to identify risks. He suggested to his coworkers where they could make improvements as a team. Sophia made sure that everyone felt heard and valued by offering them empathy and support. Emma's drive and determination motivated the team, inspiring them to set ambitious goals and work toward achieving them. Richard's deep analytical skills helped the team to make well-informed decisions. Sarah, with her focus on collaboration and harmony, helped facilitate discussions and people on the team to reach an agreement.

The Enneagram helped the team to gain insight into areas where they could improve, and where they might have blind spots. Mark learned that he had to become more flexible about his desire for perfection and that he sometimes had to accept that something was good enough, even though he thought it could still be done better. Sophia discovered it was important to set boundaries and take care of her own needs while still helping others. Emma began to realize how important teamwork was, and that she should delegate tasks. Richard attempted to share his ideas more openly, and he worked hard at collaborating with others. Sarah focused on being more assertive and expressing her insights in a way that the team took more notice of her contributions.

The team continued to use the Enneagram, and the collaboration flourished. They developed an appreciation for each other's strengths. As a team, they managed to develop a shared sense of purpose.

Clients started to notice that there was a positive change in the team's dynamic and that the quality of the work they produced had increased significantly. They gained a reputation for delivering outstanding results while encouraging a supportive environment.

Personality Tests in the Workplace

Many companies use personality tests in the workplace and when they hire new candidates. It can be a useful way for companies to discover more about their employees' cognitive abilities and technical skills.

The most common tests used are the Enneagram, the Big Five Personality Traits, and the DISC assessments.

Personality tests can also help managers adapt their style to managing their employees. It can help you understand certain things, such as if your employee will work better independently or if you should be a more hands-on manager.

You can get a better idea of how to motivate your employees in line with their personalities. The tests can also help you understand if potential new hires will fit into your team and how they will fit in.

Activity—A Combination of Personality Tests for the Workplace

It can be enlightening to use a combination of personality tests in the workplace. The tests can not only help managers learn more about potential hires or their employees, but they can also be useful for employees to get to know each other and to work together more successfully. Understanding each other's personalities can also help minimize conflict in the workplace or can ensure that conflict is resolved more successfully.

When you do this activity with a group, begin the process by explaining it to them. You should explain each test you'll be using (e.g., Enneagram, Myers-Briggs, Big Five) and inform attendees that integrating them can give them a more comprehensive view and meaningful understanding of their personalities.

You should time the activities but try to do so based on the number of people who are attending the event.

Enneagram Assessment

Distribute the Enneagram test or tell the participants where they can find it online.

Make sure that all the participants have enough time to complete the answers to the questions and that they understand what is being asked.

Collect the responses once everyone has completed the assessment.

Discussion on Enneagram Types

Explain the nine Enneagram types, their core motivations, and key characteristics.

Start the group discussion by asking the participants to share their Enneagram type, if they feel comfortable doing so. They should discuss any insights or reflections they had while learning about their Enneagram type.

More Personality Tests

Introduce one or more additional personality tests, such as the Myers-Briggs Type Indicator (MBTI) or the Big Five Personality Traits. Don't try to do too many, as it will just become confusing, and you will probably also end up running out of time.

Provide participants with access to these tests (online or printed versions) and guide them through the process of completing them.

Advise them to reflect on their own experiences and behaviors, and that they should respond honestly.

Reflection

Once all the participants have completed the relevant tests, they should complete a reflection exercise.

Encourage them to compare and contrast their results from the different tests. They should look for patterns of commonalities and differences.

Facilitate a discussion on how the insights from their Enneagram and other tests complement each other and have given them a more holistic understanding of their personalities.

Personal Growth Strategies

Encourage the participants to discuss personal growth strategies based on the combined insights from the different tests.

Facilitate a brainstorming session where participants share ideas for leveraging their strengths and addressing areas for their improvement that have been identified through the assessments.

Participants should set personal growth goals and commit to specific actions they can take moving forward.

Closure

Provide the participants with additional resources, such as recommended books or websites related to the

Enneagram and the other personality tests that were used.

You should take note that this activity should be approached with sensitivity and respect for the privacy of all the participants. While participants should be encouraged to share the results voluntarily, nobody should be forced to do so.

Practical Exercise—Enneagram Activities That Can Help You Develop Your Team

It can be a rewarding, but also challenging, experience to work with people from the different Enneagram types. Each Enneagram type can bring their unique strengths and perspectives to the work environment.

Managers can conduct a workshop or training session to introduce the Enneagram system to their teams. If the team understands the different Enneagram types and their characteristics, it can encourage understanding and empathy among the team members.

Activities

The following activities can help people understand the usefulness of knowing the different Enneagram types in the workplace:

- Each team member can do research and do a presentation on their Enneagram type's strengths and contributions. This exercise can help others appreciate the different talents people with different Enneagram types can contribute to the workplace.

- Create a map that shows the different employees' names and their Enneagram symbols. This can help you identify where people can contribute to the team according to their strengths. It will also help people understand why their coworkers might be reacting in certain ways and can make communication easier.

- Team members should also be encouraged to pair up with their coworkers who have different types for sharing sessions. They can discuss their challenges, work preferences, or strengths.

- Role-play can also encourage collaboration and problem-solving, as it encourages people to consider other people's perspectives. Try to develop scenarios that are based on normal workplace challenges.

- Team members from different types can discuss how they prefer to communicate and receive feedback in the workplace. Sharing this information can help cut down on conflict in the workplace.

- Team members should also keep journals where they consider their interactions with coworkers of different types. Reflective journaling will also promote self-awareness and will help individuals adapt their behavior for better collaboration. It will encourage them to think about their interactions with others and where they can be improved.

Key Takeaways

- The Enneagram can encourage better communication and teamwork in the workplace and can also boost productivity.

- In order to create a healthy work environment, managers need to understand the personalities and working styles of their team members.

- Understanding the Enneagram can encourage professional people to improve their communication skills.

- The Enneagram helps people gain greater self-awareness.

- Understanding the Enneagram can also help people to resolve conflict faster and more effectively in the workplace.

- Team members who don't communicate well could struggle to work together. It could be bad for business, in terms of missed deadlines and unsuccessful projects.

- The Enneagram can help organizations with professional development and growth.

- The different Enneagram types all approach their work and relationships with different strengths, motivations, and challenges.

Chapter 5:

Applying the Enneagram in Your Life

The Enneagram could be a useful tool for dealing with multiple issues in your life. It could even help you deal with mental health issues, as it did in Anne's case.

Anne's journey with the Enneagram began during a time when she was experiencing immense personal challenges. She was grappling with both mental health and physical health issues that consumed her life. Determined to find answers and regain a sense of control in her life, she turned to the Enneagram as a tool for self-discovery and healing.

When she started out with the Enneagram, Anne identified herself as a Type 9, the Peacemaker. She recognized that her tendency to avoid conflict, suppress her needs, and prioritize harmony was deeply ingrained in her personality. She also began to understand that suppressing her emotions, such as anger, was in fact making her ill. It was not only causing her mental health troubles such as anxiety and depression, but was also making her physically ill, as she had recently been diagnosed with an autoimmune disorder.

With this newfound understanding she got from the Enneagram, Anne embarked on a journey of healing during which she addressed her mental health and physical well-being with more intention and understanding.

For her mental health, Anne started therapy, and she focused on building her assertiveness skills, which helped her express her emotions and stand up for herself. She worked with her therapist to explore the underlying causes of her avoidance tendencies, which helped her to develop healthy strategies for expressing her needs and setting boundaries. Through therapy, Anne gained confidence in her voice, gradually shedding the fear of conflict, and embracing healthier forms of communication.

When it came to her physical health, Anne recognized that her tendency to neglect self-care had made her health issues worse. She usually considered herself too busy to do exercise or to take the time to make healthy meals. She learned to prioritize her well-being by establishing a consistent exercise routine, adopting a balanced diet, and improving her sleep habits. She followed the growth path for Type 9, which emphasizes self-care as part of her journey to good health.

The Enneagram also provided Anne with a framework to understand her stress responses and coping mechanisms. She discovered that as a Type 9, she often resorted to dissociation and numbing her emotions during challenging times. Armed with this awareness, she used mindfulness practices and grounding techniques to stay present and connected to her feelings. This practice of self-awareness and emotional presence helped her become more resilient.

The Enneagram served as a powerful catalyst for Anne's healing journey. It illuminated the interconnectedness between her mental and physical health, guiding her toward integrated self-care. The Enneagram helped her to prioritize her well-being in all areas of her life.

Anne's story shows that the Enneagram is a valuable tool for understanding yourself and others, and it can help you improve your relationships, also by working on your self-awareness, which is essential for better relationships.

Reasons to Learn More About Your Enneagram Type

There are many benefits to learning more about your Enneagram type.

Understanding your Enneagram type offers deep insights into your core motivations, fears, desires, and patterns of behavior. It provides a roadmap to understanding your authentic self, helping you uncover hidden aspects of your personality and gaining a clearer understanding of who you really are.

The Enneagram can help you become aware of the patterns that drive your reactions to whatever happens to you in life. This will make you understand your defense mechanisms, automatic reactions, and areas where you need to grow as a person.

Understanding your Enneagram type can also help you understand other people better and improve your relationships with them. It deepens your understanding of their perspectives, motivations, and communication styles.

Knowing more about the Enneagram can also help you deal with conflict and misunderstandings between people with different personality types. For example, something you do might anger someone from one of the other Enneagram types without you even initially realizing it.

If you understand why you've made someone angry, you can find solutions to address the conflict in a healthier way.

The Enneagram can also give you a framework for personal growth and transformation. It can tell you where you need to grow. For example, if you need to become more assertive or pay more attention to your own needs, and how you could do this by integrating the attributes from some of the other types.

A Type 9, or Peacemaker, can integrate attributes from the Type 8, the Challenger, which can include self-confidence, assertiveness, and a strong sense of personal boundaries.

The Type 9 can do this in the following ways:

- Type 9 can work on becoming more assertive and expressing their opinions and desires more directly. They can practice speaking up and setting clear boundaries even if it makes them uncomfortable at first.

- Type 9 can develop their self-confidence by recognizing and celebrating their strengths and talents. They need to recognize their own worth without relying on the validation of others.

- Type 9 can practice assertively communicating their needs and focusing on their own self-care rather than always accommodating the desires of others.

- Type 9 can stop passively going with the flow and, instead, actively take part in activities that bring them fulfillment.

By integrating these attributes from Type 8, Type 9 can experience personal growth and transformation. They learn to assert themselves and recognize their own needs.

By working on the challenges and embracing the strengths of your type, you can develop new skills, overcome limitations, and become a more integrated and whole version of yourself.

Understanding your Enneagram type can also help you figure out how you respond to stress and find better ways to cope with it. By recognizing your stress patterns and developing healthy coping mechanisms, you can improve your resilience. This knowledge can make it easier for you to deal with difficult situations while staying calm.

The Enneagram can even help you when it comes to choosing a career. By understanding your motivations and desires, you can make more informed decisions about your professional path, hobbies, and personal pursuits. This alignment leads to increased satisfaction, fulfillment, and a sense of purpose in your endeavors.

By learning more about your Enneagram type, you embark on a journey of self-discovery, which will help you reach your full potential.

Mindfulness and the Enneagram

Mindfulness is another useful tool when it comes to gaining self-awareness.

When you practice them together, they can help you get a deeper understanding of yourself, how you think, and how you relate to the world.

Practicing mindfulness involves bringing our attention to the present moment and observing our thoughts, emotions, and sensations without judgment.

Mindfulness can help us notice our automatic reactions to events and people. It's about observing our thoughts, ideas, and emotions as we have them, which can help us change our behavior in the long term. It also helps us understand how our automatic behaviors are according to our Enneagram types. This can also help us catch our behavior in the moment and behave in better ways.

Mindfulness can also help us challenge limiting beliefs we may have. Are our beliefs allowing us to grow, or are they instead limiting our growth?

How Mindfulness Helped Leila Rediscover Herself

Leila had always been identified as a Type 9 on the Enneagram, known as the Peacemaker. She usually avoided conflict and preferred safe and superficial relationships. She often found it difficult to assert herself at home and at work.

Leila realized that she wanted to make changes in her life. She wanted to achieve more at work, and she wanted healthier personal relationships. One day, she discovered the practice of mindfulness. Leila decided to use this practice during her personal growth and self-discovery process.

She started practicing mindfulness daily and felt it helped her observe her emotions and thoughts more clearly. This practice taught Leila that she tended to put others' needs before her own, and that she didn't always speak up when she disagreed about something because she wanted to keep the peace with others at all costs. She also realized that she developed this way of being in childhood. She learned at a young age that she had to please her mother, who suffered from a mental health disorder, at all times if she wanted to prevent her mother's angry outbursts.

The more Leila paid attention to her thoughts and feelings, the more she also started to realize that her Enneagram type didn't have to define her entire being. It was possible to move beyond the limitations of her Enneagram type.

Mindfulness also helped her to pause her decision-making process during difficult situations and think before she made decisions. It helped her observe her thoughts and emotions and consider the broader context before she decided to do something.

In a team meeting at work, Leila noticed that some of her coworkers weren't getting along. She would usually stay silent, but this time she managed to build the courage to express her perspective in a respectful way. To her surprise, her coworkers received her input well and her contribution sent the discussion in a more creative direction. When people opposed her views, she was also able to defend them without getting angry.

Mindfulness also helped Leila to explore her desires and passions outside of work. She enrolled in art classes and discovered that she was a talented artist. Through her practice in mindfulness, she realized that mindfulness could bring her fulfillment and help her discover greater self-awareness.

Leila also became more flexible and adaptable as she continued to practice mindfulness. She realized that she could maintain a peaceful existence without giving up on her own needs and desires. Mindfulness helped her to respond consciously and authentically.

With time, people around Leila started to notice her transformation and that she was acting in a more assertive way. Others started to see her as an inspiration, and she lived an authentic life of purpose and harmony.

How to Use the Enneagram When You Fear Personal Change

Do you feel you need to make changes to your life, but you're scared to start, or you just don't know where to start? Maybe you're indecisive and you're just not sure if you're making the right decisions. The Enneagram can help you move in the right direction.

We often need to get beyond our defense mechanisms before we can grow as people in life. Using the Enneagram can help you identify your personality type's defense mechanisms. This can help you become aware of what resistance you might be feeling as a result of your type's natural response to change, which can help you get away from automatically responding to certain issues and situations.

For example, if you're a Type 5, or Investigator, your defense mechanism is intellectualization. You could have the tendency to detach yourself from your emotions and rely on intellectual analysis. Investigators often retreat into their thoughts and put up barriers against emotional vulnerability.

If you're a Type 3, or an Achiever, your defense mechanism would be to adapt to society's expectations and prioritize the needs and desires of those around you.

You could put on a persona or suppress your authentic self to achieve success and get support from others.

The Enneagram has specific growth paths for every type. It outlines the specific paths as well as the integration points for each type. The paths provide you with areas for your personal development that can help you overcome your fear of growing.

For example, if you're a Perfectionist, your growth path would be to embrace the qualities of the Type 7, the Enthusiast. The integration point is when you become like the Type 7 by being more joyful and open-minded. You've learned to embrace your imperfections and let go of your tendency to excessively criticize yourself.

The Enneagram's wing types and stress/security points can give you insight into the various facets of your personality. Exploring the characteristics of these adjacent types can help you see how you could express qualities from the neighboring types. By integrating the qualities from your wings or using the strengths of your stress/security points, you can become more flexible and resilient.

The Enneagram encourages you to grow in the direction of the integration for each type. You can counteract your resistance and fear by consciously embracing the positive qualities associated with your integration point. For example, if you are a Type 5, moving toward the healthy qualities of Type 8 (integration point), such as assertiveness and self-confidence, can help you navigate your personal growth challenges.

The Enneagram will teach you to have compassion and self-acceptance by helping you understand that your fears, resistance, and defensive patterns are adaptive responses that have served you in the past.

The Enneagram Can Help You Identify and Release Patterns of Self-Judgment and Negative Self-Talk

Since the Enneagram can help you become more self-aware by giving insight into your motivations, fears, and defense mechanisms, it will also assist you in becoming aware of your negative self-talk. You can begin to recognize your automatic negative thoughts and beliefs and understand how they relate to your Enneagram type's core motivations.

Each Enneagram type has an inner critic that judges and criticizes. The Enneagram can help you recognize your inner critic and the way in which it manifests for your type. If you can recognize it as a conditioned pattern, you can distance yourself from its influence and challenge its validity. You will start to notice when you're having these overly critical thoughts, which can be driven by fear. When you have this awareness, you can reframe negative thoughts and replace them with more balanced and compassionate views.

Developing a Personalized Enneagram-Based Personal Growth Plan: Tools and Resources

You can create your own Enneagram growth plan vehicle using certain tools and resources.

These are some of the resources that are available:

- There are several books that provide in-depth insight into the Enneagram. Some popular titles include *The Wisdom of the Enneagram* by Don Richard Riso and Russ Hudson, *The Road Back to You* by Ian Morgan Cron and Suzanne Stabile, and *Personality Types* by Don Richard Riso.

- If you're an Enneagram enthusiast, there are also several websites that you can visit to obtain more information. The Enneagram Institute (www.enneagraminstitute.com) offers detailed descriptions about each type and advice for growth.

- An Enneagram assessment can also help you identify your type. Various online assessments are available, including on the website of The Enneagram Institute. You may have to pay for some of these tests, but there are also free versions available. The Riso-Hudson Enneagram Type Indicator (RHETI) and The

Enneagram Institute's online test are two of the more commonly used tests. The assessments shouldn't be regarded as 100% accurate, but they can give you insight and guide you toward further research.

- You should consider attending retreats or workshops that focus on the Enneagram. These events are useful, as you can learn from the Enneagram experts who facilitate them, as well as other people who attend them. You'll also be able to take part in exercises that allow you to explore your type.

- An Enneagram coach or therapist can provide you with personalized guidance and support. They can help you understand your type and develop strategies for personal growth.

- Journaling about your Enneagram type can help you gain insight into your triggers, patterns, and growth. This can also help you identify what might be standing in the way of your personal growth.

Using the Enneagram in Conjunction with Other Tests

You can use the Enneagram in conjunction with other tests to explore your personality. It's often useful to use different assessments to shed light on the complexities of your personality.

Using multiple frameworks can give you a more comprehensive and nuanced understanding of your personality. It can also enhance your journey to true self-awareness and make your personal growth journey more meaningful and interesting.

Different tests can help us explore different aspects of our character, behavior, and values. For example, if we use the Enneagram with assessments like the MBTI or the Big Five Personality Traits, we can gain insight into both the cognitive and emotional dimensions of our personality.

Myers-Briggs Type Indicator

The MBTI categorizes people into different personality types based on four key preferences:

- **extraversion (E) or introversion (I)**: Do you get your energy from being around other people and external stimulation (extraversion) or from being alone and reflecting on your thoughts (introversion)?

- **sensing (S) or intuition (N):** How do you gather information and process details? Sensing people focus on concrete facts and the present moment, while intuitive people tend to focus on patterns, possibilities, and future implications.

- **thinking (T) or feeling (F):** This indicates how you make decisions. Thinking people prioritize logic and objective analysis, while feeling people consider emotions and personal values when they make decisions.

- **judging (J) or perceiving (P):** How do you deal with the outside world and organize your life? Judging people prefer structure, planning, and making decisions, while perceiving people are flexible, adaptable, and open to new possibilities.

By combining these preferences, the MBTI indicates 16 different personality types, such as INFJ, ENFP, or INTJ. Each type represents a unique combination of these preferences, which gives insight into how people make decisions and interact with others.

Big Five Personality Traits

The Five-Factor Model breaks down personality into five key dimensions or traits:

- **openness:** People who score high on this trait tend to be imaginative, adventurous, and willing to try new things. Those who score low usually prefer routine and familiarity.

- **conscientiousness:** This trait relates to how organized, responsible, and disciplined a person is. Those who score high are usually diligent, reliable, and goal-oriented. Low scorers are often more spontaneous and flexible.

- **extraversion:** Extroverts enjoy being around people, and they are energized by social interactions. Introverts prefer to be on their own and need quiet time to recharge.

- **agreeableness:** This trait reflects how friendly, cooperative, and compassionate someone is. High scorers are often kind, empathetic, and willing to help others. People who score low could be more skeptical and competitive.

- **neuroticism:** This trait is about how prone someone is to experiencing negative emotions. High scorers could be more anxious, moody, and easily stressed. Low scorers tend to be calmer and more emotionally resilient.

The Big Five traits exist on a continuum, and everyone possesses a unique combination of scores across the five dimensions.

Understanding the Big Five traits can provide you with insight on how to interact with others and how to handle life in general and make decisions. It will also give you a better understanding of different personalities.

The Enneagram and other personality assessments ultimately complement each other, and they weave together a tapestry of insights that will guide you toward greater self-understanding, empathy, and personal growth.

The Enneagram could complement other personality tests in the following ways:

- Combining the Enneagram with other personality tests can offer different perspectives and insights into various aspects of a person's personality. Each tool may focus on different aspects such as cognitive functions, behavioral tendencies, or values, providing a more holistic understanding.

- If you have taken other personality tests and received specific results, exploring the Enneagram can help validate or provide further confirmation of your personality type. It can offer a different framework for understanding your motivations, fears, and growth opportunities.

- Personality tests often categorize individuals into specific types or traits, while the Enneagram delves deeper into the underlying motivations and core beliefs that influence behavior. Combining both approaches can provide a more nuanced understanding of personality by integrating broader traits with more detailed insights.

- Integrating the Enneagram with other personality assessments can enhance personal growth and development efforts. By identifying patterns and tendencies from different angles, people can develop a more meaningful understanding of their strengths, areas for improvement, and potential paths for growth.

It's important to approach the integration of different personality tests with an open mind and recognize that no single assessment can fully capture the complexity of a person.

It's vital to remember that the Enneagram is a dynamic system that recognizes the potential for growth and change of each person.

Activity—Building Your Own Enneagram Growth Plan

For this exercise, you just need your journal, or you could write on one of your electronic devices.

Before you write anything down, you're first going to do some reflection for this exercise.

Reflection

Start by reflecting on your core Enneagram type. If you haven't chosen one yet, read about the nine types and then choose one that you think sounds the most like you.

Read a detailed description of your Enneagram type to get a deeper understanding of your fears and desires.

Think about patterns and tendencies you could have noticed in your thoughts and behavior.

Growth Areas

Identify areas in your life where you would like to focus on personal growth. This could be related to your Enneagram type's blind spots or challenges you want to overcome.

Growth Goals

Set goals for the areas that you identified in the previous step.

You could set your goals by making use of specific, measurable, attainable, relevant, and time-bound (SMART) goals.

Planning

Brainstorm actions you could take to work toward your growth goals. These actions should be aligned with your Enneagram type's patterns.

Consider both inner work (such as self-reflection, mindfulness practices, or therapy) and outer work (such as seeking support, learning new skills, or engaging in relevant activities).

Break your actions down into smaller steps and create a timeline or action plan that shows how you will work on each step.

Self-Accountability

You need to be self-accountable in your personal growth. Review your progress regularly, track your actions, and assess your growth toward your goals.

Write your reflections and achievements in your journal.

Reflection and Commitment

Think about your growth journey and the benefits you envision for yourself.

Make a commitment to yourself that you're willing to embrace personal growth and transformation.

This practical activity will help you take ownership of your personal growth within the context of the Enneagram. Revisit your growth plan regularly as you progress on your journey.

Key Takeaways

- There are many benefits to learning more about your Enneagram type.

- The Enneagram provides you with a roadmap to understanding your authentic self and uncovering hidden aspects of your personality.

- The Enneagram can help you become aware of the patterns that influence your reactions to what happens to you. It can also help you see where you need to grow as a person.

- If you know more about the Enneagram, you'll be better able to deal with conflicts and misunderstandings between people with different personality types.

- Understanding your Enneagram type can also help you understand how you respond to stress and find better ways to deal with it.

- You can improve your resilience by managing your stress levels and developing healthy coping mechanisms.

- If you practice mindfulness and the Enneagram together, they can help you gain a deeper understanding of yourself and how you deal with the world.

- Mindfulness can help you to focus on the present moment and to observe your thoughts, feelings, and sensations without judging yourself.

- Mindfulness can also help you take note of your automatic reactions to people and events.

- The Enneagram can help you make important changes to your life.

- The Enneagram can help you move beyond your defense mechanisms to start making positive changes to your life.

- It's a great idea to develop your own personalized Enneagram-based personal growth plan. There are websites, books, and workshops available that can help you with doing this.

- An Enneagram coach can also help you with personalized support.

Conclusion

I hope that studying the Enneagram has given you the tools you needed to build bridges to those difficult but essential people in your life. I trust that it has helped you uncover some of the intricacies of human nature.

What probably fascinated you the most was uncovering the patterns and behavior that you struggled to understand in the people closest to you. You would have unraveled the types of people in your life one by one. You might have been amazed to find that suddenly their actions and behavior, which you used to find strange, started to make sense to you. The behavior of your friend, who is a Type 3, and always striving for recognition and success, now makes complete sense to you for the first time.

General behaviors become less annoying, and you can give your family and friends the support they need.

You can approach people with a deeper understanding and more compassion. You're now able to see beyond a surface-level argument with people, and you realize why their fears and desires have led to the argument. Instead of hitting back at them, you can take a step back and empathize with them.

The Enneagram won't only have given you tools to understand others but will also help you develop your own growth path. You can now recognize the areas in your life where you need to make improvements.

When it comes to highlights, this book would have taught you more about the following: It informed you about the fears, motivations and desires that shaped your behaviors, thoughts, and emotions. The more your self-awareness grows, the more you will see where you need to transform your life.

The Enneagram would have taught you about empathy, compassion, and acceptance. It's important to remember that our Enneagram type's patterns and challenges are not flaws, but rather adaptive strategies we developed to navigate life.

The Enneagram also illuminated our relationship dynamics. The book revealed how the different types interact with each other, indicating potential areas of conflict and areas where growth is needed.

I also want to encourage you to stay open-minded and curious as you delve into the Enneagram. You should approach self-reflection with a sense of wonder and be willing to uncover the hidden layers of your personality.

You should embrace the uncomfortable, as this is where you will find your true growth. Growth is usually outside our comfort zones. We need to embrace the discomfort that goes along with self-discovery, and we should be willing to confront and change the patterns and limitations of our Enneagram types.

When and where can you engage and join with others who are interested in the Enneagram? Take part in workshops, online communities, and discussion groups, as this will help you gain new perspectives and insights.

The Enneagram also empowers you when it comes to finding common ground with others. It can help us realize that even though we're different, we have shared ideas and fears. Our shared values and aspirations can help us build better, more empathetic relationships.

We encourage you to continue using the Enneagram as your guide along this transformative journey. It's entirely possible to take your relationships, and your life, to the next level while using the Enneagram.

Unlock Your Bonus! – Enneagram Cheat Sheet

Thank you for embarking on a journey with *"The Enneagram Code"*! As a token of our appreciation and to further enrich your understanding, we're offering a gift, an Enneagram cheat sheet delineating each of the nine Enneagram types.

Keep this essential guide at hand for quick and easy reference as you uncover the fascinating world of Enneagram personalities for yourself and those around you.

To claim your gift, point your camera at the QR code and follow the link.

It's time to go deeper into the enneagram codes.

Enjoy the journey of discovery!

Your Feedback Matters to Us

If you've enjoyed discovering *"The Enneagram Code"*. We'd love to hear more about your experience.

Your insights and opinions can help others delve into the magic of Enneagrams and empower their personal growth journey just like you.

Whether it's a standout moment you've had or a transformation you've experienced, your words matter – and we can't wait to read them.

Thank you for sharing your Enneagram journey with us.

Eden Storm

About the Author

Eden Storm is a self-help and personal transformation coach, who brings a refreshing and unique perspective to understanding oneself and others. Eden's dedication to research and her genuine interest in helping others has positioned her as a trusted professional in the field.

With a passionate pursuit of knowledge and an insatiable curiosity, Eden has spent extensive time exploring human behavior, psychology, and emotional intelligence. This wealth of research, combined with her innate empathy, allows her to decode complex emotions and unravel the intricacies of interpersonal connections.

Through her profound insights, she empowers individuals to embark on transformative journeys towards self-discovery and personal fulfillment.

Beyond her writing, Eden finds solace in various personal hobbies and interests. She derives immense joy from immersing herself in nature, practicing mindfulness and meditation, and exploring new cultures through travel. These pursuits not only fuel her creativity but also provide her with valuable insights into the human experience.

As a trusted and respected voice in the self-help genre, Eden Storm invites you to join her transformative journey towards self-discovery, personal growth, and a profoundly enriched life.

References

Christian, K. (2020, January 29). *How to cultivate healthier relationships based on your Enneagram type*. The Good Trade. https://www.thegoodtrade.com/features/enneagram-in-relationships/

Cloete, D. (2010). *Origins and history of the Enneagram*. Integrative. https://www.integrative9.com/enneagram/history/

Daniels, D. (n.d.). *History of the Enneagram as we know it today*. David N. Daniels, M.D. https://drdaviddaniels.com/history-of-the-enneagram-we-know-today/

Doyle, E. (2022, November 14). *Enneagram 9: The Peacemaker*. Cloverleaf. https://cloverleaf.me/blog/enneagram-type-9-the-peacemaker/

Doyle, E. (2022, May 9). *Enneagram subtypes. Helpful guide to 3 instinctual variants*. https://enneagramgift.com/enneagram-subtypes/

The Enneagram Institute. (2014). *The traditional Enneagram (History)*.

https://www.enneagraminstitute.com/the-traditional-enneagram

4 powerful ways the Enneagram can improve work culture. (2022, May 11). *FormAssembly*. https://www.formassembly.com/blog/enneagram-workplace-benefits/

Harris, E. (2023, March 1). *5 reasons to learn more about your Enneagram type*. Truity. https://www.truity.com/blog/5-reasons-learn-more-about-your-enneagram-type

Integrative9. (n.d.). *Enneagram type 1 personality - The Reformer*. Strict Perfectionist Description. https://www.integrative9.com/enneagram/introduction/type-1

Intro to the Enneagram. (n.d.). *What are the 9 personality types?* YouTube. https://www.youtube.com/watch?v=cCP0Vn4d0CI

Molly Owens. (2019, August 8). *What is the Enneagram of personality?* Truity. https://www.truity.com/enneagram/what-is-enneagram

The Narrative Enneagram. (2019). *Enneagram instinctual subtypes*. https://www.narrativeenneagram.org/instinctual-subtypes/

Rush to Press. (2020, March 9). *Brené Brown pens foreword to "The Enneagram of Belonging" by renowned*

Enneagram expert Chris Heuertz. https://rushtopress.org/6333-2/

Storm, S. (2019, December 2). *Myers-Briggs® and the Enneagram - What's the same and what's different?* Psychology Junkie. https://www.psychologyjunkie.com/myers-briggs-and-the-enneagram-whats-the-same-and-whats-different/

TestGorilla. (2021, June 20). *How should you use personality tests in the workplace?* https://www.testgorilla.com/blog/personality-tests-workplace/

Wong, K. (2019, May 31). *Top 10 free Enneagram tests.* The Millennial Grind. https://millennial-grind.com/top-10-best-enneagram-tests/

Printed in Great Britain
by Amazon